Jorge Prieto-Arguelles, circa 1938

The Quarterback Who Almost Wasn't

Jorge Prieto

Houston, Texas
1994

This book is made possible through support from the National Endowment for the Arts (a federal agency), the Lila Wallace-Reader's Digest fund and the Andrew W. Mellow Foundation.

Arte Público Press
University of Houston
Houston, Texas 77204-2090

Cover design by Gladys Ramírez

Prieto, Jorge
The quarterback who almost wasn't / Jorge Prieto.
p. cm.
ISBN 1-55885-109-7 : $9.95
1. Prieto, Jorge. 2. Football players—United States—Biography. 3. Heart—Diseases—Patients—Biography. 4. Physicians—United States—Biography I. Title.
GV939.P75A3 1994
796.332'092—dc20
[B] 93-29314
CIP

The paper used in this publication meets the requirements of the American National Standard for Permanence of Paper for Printed Library Materials Z39.48-1984. ∞

The Quarterback Who Almost Wasn't

Estadio de la Ciudad de los Deportes, circa 1945
(Mexico City Sports Stadium, circa 1945)

It was the early autumn of 1929 in Los Angeles, California, when a young Mexican boy sat on a curbside watching fascinated while older neighborhood boys played a strange game. In the middle of the street, some neighborhood kids were throwing and kicking an oblong-shaped leather ball. I was that awestruck boy. I had been living with my family in different parts of the Southwest for the previous five years.

I was born in Mexico City, but my family moved to Texas when my father became a political exile in 1923. Now we were settled (at least for the time being) in California, and I was watching in wonder as my neighbors threw long, arching spirals with a football. The graceful flight of that oblong leather ball seemed a thing of beauty to me.

There was only one Mexican family in that neighborhood of people in modest or poor circumstances. What I knew was that my family was "different" because we were from Mexico, and this was not our permanent home. For years I was to live with the idea that we were destined, "God willing," to return to Mexico. My mother kept that hope alive at the same time that she taught us to respect

our father. She convinced us that he was a great man who was suffering an unjust exile as a matter of principle, and that he was destined to return home soon. All this was due to a conflict she called "La Revolución," a conflict in which my father had participated. Being eleven years old in 1929, I naturally didn't understand all this. I understood that I was different from most of the neighborhood people. All I had to do was look at my brown skin and realize the difference. But I spoke the same language as my neighbors, went to the same school, and decided to participate in the same games.

It would be many years before that area, near the University of Southern California, became an all-Mexican neighborhood, a "barrio." Meanwhile, I was getting acquainted with all sorts of new things, such as American sports. In the fall of 1929, I was simply a happy youngster discovering the wonders of a new game. Each time that ball went spiraling through the air, I marveled. I became determined to learn how to pass and kick a football the way my neighbors were doing. Fortunately for me, one of those neighbors, John Worth, took a friendly liking to me and started teaching me how to throw and kick that strange ball. He also gave me a nickname. He started calling me "Chili Beans." I didn't exactly like it, because it seemed to make me too different from the rest of the neighborhood kids. I preferred my Christian name of Jorge, but they had trouble pronouncing it. And John Worth insisted that I was full of pepper, just like a chili bean. The name stuck. It mattered little to me, as long as I was able to play with the older neighborhood boys on their football team.

I was almost the smallest boy on that team, but I won my way in. That Los Angeles neighborhood had people

from everywhere. On our side of the street there were two Irish and two German families with only one boy in my age group. Across the street, there were two Italian families—the Barsuglis and the Magentis—and each one had a couple of boys that were my main rivals. They were bigger and could run faster than I could, but I was determined to be quarterback on the football team and catcher on the baseball team. There was a French-Canadian family just north of us and the Schaeffers at the head of an alley, half-a-block north. I learned how to eat gefilte fish at the Schaeffer's, and I taught Irving, the only Jewish boy in the neighborhood, how to eat *frijoles* (pinto beans). The rest of the houses didn't have any children, and so I don't remember anything about them except that my mother told me that "Americans" were a strange people who frequently had no children.

Fortunately, there were enough young boys about my age to make up either football or baseball teams, according to the season. It took more than one fist fight for me to get on those teams, but those were mostly due to racism and not to sports ability. When I was first accepted on the football team, I was so happy that it didn't matter that I was only a lineman. In those days, the best players were always in the backfield. Being on the team was good enough for me, at the time.

There was probably never a more ragged team than ours: the Silver Lake neighborhood team of 1929. We didn't have a single helmet to our name. Our shoulder pads were made from rags that had been folded over and sewn to our cheap grey jerseys. My mother had the natural fears that most mothers have about injuries in football, but she not only sewed on padding for my shoulders, she made me

the strongest knee pads ever. She saw the enthusiasm I had for that sport and not only overcame her fears, but even encouraged me to play. She already knew I was getting into many fist fights and must have thought that if I excelled at any sport, my race would become irrelevant—as it did. Of course, those fights were due to racism. Ours was the only Mexican family in that neighborhood, and I was the only one in our family who wanted to play in every sport our neighbors were playing. The first fight was at the entrance to the alley just north of our house. One Saturday morning, Art Magenti and Nick Barsugli—the biggest and reputedly the toughest boys in the neighborhood—stood at the head of that alley and said, "No greaser can come in here."

I replied that I was on my way to Silver Lake playground to a Boy Scout meeting and that I was coming through that alley. Nick Barsugli put a piece of wood on his shoulder and dared me to knock if off. I knew what that meant and I felt scared. I had never had a fist fight before and I knew that it was important that I make at least a good show. And so I knocked that chip off of Barsugli's shoulder and advanced on him with my fists flying. Our Lady of Guadalupe must have been watching over me that day because I gave Barsugli a pretty good thrashing. Not that I believe that the Virgin Mary actually sponsors fighters, but faith in her protection had already been deeply ingrained in me.

That day I didn't really have much time for religious thoughts, just the need to survive and excel that most young men feel when challenged. I bloodied Nick Barsugli's nose and won my right, forevermore, to go through that alley on Occidental Boulevard. There were other chal-

lenges and fights at the school playgrounds. Both at my grammar school, the Micheltorena Street School, and later at Thomas Starr King Junior High, I had to use my fists to win the right to play.

After the first fight on each playground, I was rarely challenged again. The kids found out I wasn't ever willing to back down. I also became good at every sport, and so those fights became very infrequent.

My first game of regular tackle football is still fresh in my memory. The vacant sandlot we were to play on was full of rocks and broken glass. We had to spend a good while before the game just getting rid of the biggest rocks and as much of the broken glass as possible. Then it came time to line up for my first kickoff. That was "the moment of truth" as Spaniards say when facing a fierce bull. I felt a mixture of fear and desire to survive victorious. I was smaller than most of my teammates and had never made a tackle. I was as worried of making a mistake as I was of physical injury. I was the only Mexican on the field and very conscious of that fact. I had to prove my courage, as well as my ability to play football.

My fears all seemed to disappear when I made my first tackle. I had been placed at left end, and the first time our opponents had the ball they ran the play right at me. It seemed to me as if their entire team was running interference for their ball-carrier. I was expected to stop him. And to my amazement I did, right on the line of scrimmage. From that moment on, I felt the excitement of the game and not the pain of the blows. I also caught a pass for a short gain that brought us close to their goal for the first time in the game. We scored on the next play and I felt almost a hero. I enjoyed that game as much as any young-

ster ever enjoyed football.

In those days, very few passes were thrown and fewer were completed. So, suddenly, I was a success. Gone was the fear of losing the game because of a mistake, and gone, too, was the fear of getting hurt. I was a football player. At least, I thought so.

After that first victory, I also ceased to worry about my rather small size. Being one of the smaller players on the team had not made any difference. We only had two more games to play that fall, and we won both. So I began to dream.

Our coach was a neighbor by the name of John Worth. He was a substitute halfback on the University of Southern California varsity football team, and we naturally looked up to him. He was both the neighborhood athletic hero and our coach. Whenever I saw him home from school or football practice, I hounded him to teach me how to pass. I knew that backfield players could be smaller than linemen, and I desperately wanted to learn how to throw those long arching spirals that had first attracted me to the game. That U.S.C. player was a very friendly fellow and he taught me the basics of football. He also became, unknown to him, the source of my determination to someday play college football.

One day I asked my mentor if he thought I could ever play for U.S.C. He laughed good-naturedly and told me that such was impossible because that university did not accept Blacks or Mexicans into their school. When I asked him about U.C.L.A. or Stanford, I got the same discouraging answer. Another neighbor and friend, George LaPorte, a French-Canadian about my same age, overheard that conversation with John Worth. He noticed my dismay and

told me that there was a little school back east in a town called South Bend, and that it was a Catholic University and, therefore, would almost surely accept Mexicans because of our religion. He also told me that the school he was talking about was called The University of Notre Dame, that it had good football teams, and that it was going to play against U.S.C. that very weekend in the Los Angeles Coliseum.

John Worth told us that Notre Dame was sure to lose because it had only been able to defeat Northwestern by 14 to 0 and West Point by a mere 7 to 6 score. Also, Notre Dame was missing its first- and second-string fullbacks and would have to use an untested substitute. Since U.S.C. had defeated Stanford by more than 40 points and the University of California-Berkeley, also by a very large margin, it looked pretty bad for that Catholic school. The odds were against Notre Dame, but my mother said we would pray for victory and surely win. Since neither George LaPorte nor I had enough money for tickets to the Coliseum, we would hear the game on the radio.

That Saturday my friend George, my mother and I were hanging onto every word spoken by the radio announcer. My mother, of course, had her Rosary beads in her hands, and I could hear her murmured prayers. It seems as if I can still hear and feel the excitement in the announcer's voice when he said . . . "the Irish are out of the huddle . . . they are up to the line of scrimmage and they shift to the right. The ball goes to the new fullback, O'Connor, and he cuts inside the Trojan left end . . . he's past the line of scrimmage . . . he is going five, ten yards, and he has broken into the clear . . . only the safetyman can stop him, but O'Conner is too fast for him and it looks

like he is going to go all the way for a touchdown. He is crossing the goal line . . . An 80 yard run for a touchdown!!" That was the decisive play of the game. Frank Carideo had already scored with a surprise pass from Marchmont Schwartz very early in the game. We were more than joyful as Notre Dame went on to win that Saturday by a score of 27 to 0.

That was the last game under Coach Knute Rockne. An airplane crash the following spring turned Rockne from a very successful coach into an almost mythical legend. His last victory made me believe the impossible: that I could someday enroll at that university. That Saturday my mother and I came to know, for the first time, what "the spirit of Notre Dame" was all about. It was about overcoming great obstacles. They were expected to lose and they won. My mother was so happy that glorious autumn afternoon that she went to the neighborhood stores on Sunset Boulevard and bought two sweat shirts. She had asked me about the Notre Dame colors—which I knew from the newspapers and from the radio announcer to be blue and gold—and had also bought some dye. She then proceeded to give me one of the best gifts of my life. She dyed those sweat shirts blue—one for my brother Guillermo and one for me—and sewed big intertwined N and D yellow cloth letters across the chest. My brother was only ten years old and wasn't much impressed, but I went out with my blue and gold shirt feeling very much a part of Notre Dame.

My mother could not know, naturally, how valuable that happy memory would become. She was to use that incident seven years later to challenge me to continue wanting to live when my life seemed to have become

entirely hopeless.

Meanwhile, I was one of the happiest youngsters in our neighborhood. I lived up to my nickname of "Chili Beans" by taking part in every game of any sport that my friends and schoolmates played. All was not sports, however. My mother wisely introduced me to public libraries like the Santa Monica library, where I was free to read any book I wished. For me, the wonder was that I could actually take a bunch of books home. Six was the number limit allowed, if I remember correctly. My mother saw to it that there was some balance by allowing me only three books on sports. That's how I came to learn a great deal about aviation and about the history of the United States.

At the same time, she and my father saw to it that my brother and I learned something about our Mexican heritage. They had a relative bring up the twelve volumes of a Spanish encyclopedia titled *El Tesoro de la Juventud* (The Treasure of Youth). I remember believing that those books contained all of human knowledge. They had a great deal of poetry and my mother would read those poems to us after supper and have us repeat them. We received the knowledge and learned the sounds of Spanish. But we did not learn how to write it. My mother had her hands full with eight children and a demanding husband, and was too busy to teach us to write. My father had to work long hours in order to make ends meet. I have no idea how my mother was ever able to take the time to have us recite Spanish poetry.

Many years later I taught my two youngest daughters to read Spanish in the same way. Margarita and Lupita learned the Spanish language through the poetry of Ruben Darío, Gabriela Mistral and Pablo Neruda. While reading

these poets with my daughters, I felt again the love that my mother had lavished on her children in Los Angeles. I came to understand what the great Spanish poet Juan Ramón Jimínez meant when he wrote that, in traveling through the countryside with Platero, his donkey, he lived "hours infected by eternity." Such were the hours spent hearing my two daughters recite Spanish poetry with their soft, sweet voices.

I was an above average student during our years in California, but my greatest interest was sports. I also had a newspaper and a magazine route. After school, I would load my bicycle—bought, literally, dime by dime—with the Los Angeles *Herald-Express* and set out to deliver it to about 50 or 60 customers. This was just before the Wall-Street crash of 1929. The impact of that did not become noticeable to me until about the middle of 1931, when the number of people willing to spend 5 cents on a paper dropped to less than a dozen. They also stopped buying the magazine, *The Saturday Evening Post*. I could never understand why, with that name, the magazine always came out on Thursdays. Neither could I understand the lack of courtesy of so many that didn't give me a chance to tell them anything about the magazine but simply shut the door in my face. I went from door to door trying to sell that magazine with the Norman Rockwell covers from 1929 to 1933. In the process I learned something about overcoming discouragement. When I returned with unsold copies, my mother would always encourage me by saying that the next week would be better. But, the diminishing number of customers for the magazine made me give up that route early in 1933. Without the magazine route, my brother Guillermo and I had to take on additional work.

We arranged to deliver the Sunday edition of the *Los Angeles Times*. On Saturday afternoons and on Sunday mornings my brother and I would load two large wooden crates and set out to deliver about two-hundred newspapers each weekend. That meant pulling or pushing those big crates with large metal wheels rimmed by thin rubber tires up and down the seemingly endless hills of the Sunset Boulevard and Silver Lake neighborhoods. On Sundays we got up at dawn in order to put those thick newspapers together. We each had about fifty customers on Saturdays and another fifty on Sundays. Even our early starts did not enable us to get back home on time to go to the noon Mass with the rest of the family.

My father was working such long hours that we saw little of him except on weekends. Even in his absence, his authority was always present to us in a very positive way. My mother had explained how his exile was a courageous, almost noble thing. He had given up great political power by facing up to the President of Mexico in public. Ordinarily, being in exile is considered a negative thing, a failure. In our case, my mother saw to it that we understood that my father's exile was something to be proud of. I remember her showing me a picture of Victor Hugo in that Spanish-language encyclopedia. He was draped in a long flowing robe and standing on the cliffs of Dover, looking across the English Channel towards his beloved France. She made us equate Victor Hugo's sacrifice in his opposition to French tyranny with my father's opposition to a Mexican President who had betrayed the Revolution by designating his successor instead of holding an election.

That conviction made it possible for me to understand my father's occasional explosions of rage. It taught

me that integrity was more important than success. It also made my fights against racial slurs easier to tolerate.

My sense of values was reinforced when my father, who was working many more hours a week than the average, gave up his Sunday morning rest in order to see that we made it to Mass on time. From 1930 to the end of his exile in June of 1933, my father gave up his Sunday rest. He would get up with us before dawn, help us load our papers into his little Chevrolet, and drive us up and down those hills to deliver our newspapers. After that, the whole family went to church together. I began to appreciate the mystic beauty of the ancient liturgy of mass. It was in Latin, of course, but both parents would translate it for the three oldest children.

Religion and literature were not the only tools my parents used to develop our sense of values. They encouraged me to join the Boy Scouts, even though they were never able to afford the uniform. I became a member of the Raccoon Patrol of Troop 336, Boy Scouts of America. That scout group was based at my own Micheltorena Street School, and it gave me my first opportunity to go camping. In the summer of 1932, I was able to go camping with my Troop up in the hills north of Los Angeles. I burned my fingers trying to cook my own meals, rolled out of my tent during the night because I had foolishly set the tent on a narrow ridge, and learned to enjoy swimming. I have loved the outdoor wilderness ever since. I didn't have the uniform, but I had everything else a Scout needed: I took the oath and the recommendations of my Boy Scout Handbook seriously. To this day, my brothers and sisters make jokes about my dashing off to wash my hands as soon as anybody says that we are about to have a meal.

With my patrol, I also had my first brush with the reality of death. One of my best Scout friends cut his leg on something sharp and developed what they called "blood poisoning." This was long before penicillin, and my friend died when his life was just starting. Somehow my mother found the money to buy me a Scout hat, and with that and my neckerchief, I looked enough like a Scout to attend the funeral at the old Hollywood Hills Cemetery. That was the first time in my life that death became a nearby reality. The haunting notes of our bugler blowing "Taps" as we laid our friend into the earth have ever since reminded me of the solemnity of death. That death helped me to understand the value of love. A friend I cared for had suddenly gone from my life.

I had already come to appreciate the meaning of love from my mother's constant encouragement to study and learn, from her support for my love of football, and especially from her sewing of the yellow letters N and D on my blue jersey. My father had, naturally, much less contact with us, but he seemed to know almost everything we did or were interested in. In contrast to my mother, he liked my getting into so many fist fights. I am not sure why, but he seemed to think that it was good that I had to fight my way in and out of alleys and school yards.

My father participated in my education in a unique way, a way that influenced my final choice of vocation. During the last two years of his exile, he had two different jobs. One was as an announcer on a Spanish-language radio station in Bakersfield and the other was in the distribution and sale of brooms and small bags of coffee to the innumerable little grocery stores in the Mexican communities.

Since Mexicans were already a major part of the labor force in California agriculture, this meant that he traveled up and down southern California. And he sometimes took me with him. Southern California in those years was full of orange groves as well as fields with other fruits, such as grapes. He made me notice that the field hands gathering those abundant harvests were almost all Mexicans.

I recall that the Depression was so bad that he frequently came back to the car without having sold a single bag of coffee or a single broom to the store he went into. I realize now how strong he was, because I do not recall ever hearing any expression of despair from him. Anger at "the Gringos" was very frequently voiced by him, but never despair. My mother explained that his anger was really directed at the United States government for having intervened against the Mexican Revolution. She also convinced us that we should not have that same anger since that was over and done with and that only a few powerful politicians were guilty, not "the Gringos," as we were hearing. This distinction was fundamental for all eight children, especially for me since I was destined to live most of my life in the United States.

I further learned about generosity when my father found time to drive me to a downtown lumber yard to find balsa wood for the model airplanes I was trying to build. That wood was so expensive in the local hardware stores that, without his effort in taking me to that distant lumber yard, my joy of building and flying those rubberband powered airplanes would have ended. He lived until 1990 and gave us some almost incredible examples of courage and generosity. But what he did for his son in 1930 is one of

the important lessons of my life. He was a political legend to all who knew the Mexican Revolution of 1910-1924. To us he was a firm, warm and generous father.

Many children seem to believe that the parent that works knows little, if anything, about their interests. I too thought my father was ignorant of my particular interest in football, and especially of my interest in the University of Notre Dame. I found out otherwise early in 1931. I was walking with him down Olvera Street in downtown Los Angeles when he suddenly stopped and said, "Look, son, that coach from Notre Dame died." He was pointing at a newspaper headline that announced the death of Knute Rockne in an airplane crash in Kansas. Until that moment I had believed that my dad neither knew nor cared about football. His generation in Mexico had grown up participating in a great armed struggle and with very little time or interest for sports. Nevertheless, Jorge Prieto Laurens was one revolutionary who knew what interested his children.

Political exile is essentially different from immigration. It is forced, dangerous and indefinite. It naturally provokes anger and even moments of despair. My parents hid their despair from us. For my father it must have been as difficult as it was for Victor Hugo, the great French writer-poet of the nineteenth century. It was all the more difficult since my father was forced to live in the country whose government had frozen all attempts at significant social reforms in Mexico. Fortunately, he was one of those unusually vigorous men who are never truly defeated. His vigor was physical, intellectual and spiritual. Otherwise, he would not have survived the ten years in the United States in the way he did. He and my mother never lost their good humor, just as they never lost their determina-

tion to return to Mexico. At the time I did not understand why my mother made us hide the comic pages of the American newspapers when my father was about to come home. She would pull out the comic pages of a newspaper called *La Opinion* or *La Prensa* and make my father believe we were interested in reading in Spanish, which of course we were not.

My mother knew that there was no way of telling how prolonged that exile could become and that my father feared that we would lose our love for Mexico if we lost the language. After all, the government of Mexico was supported by the White House and by the wealthy Americans and British that owned the vast oil fields of Mexico. Her fear of a prolonged exile was lessened by trying to make sure that my father saw signs of hope in our interest about everything Mexican, even the comic strips of newspapers.

The trials of a politician's wife are painful enough in ordinary settings. Our exile into a land considered by most Mexicans as an enemy tested all the virtues and character traits of both our parents. Exile, a large family and, finally, the Great Depression of 1929 tested Don Jorge and Doña Felisa to the limits of human endurance. We were always poor in possessions but not in spirit, since all of us eight children enjoyed life so much during those California years. My mother later told me that she too enjoyed the exile because my father was in less danger. But he was not entirely out of danger since the President of Mexico sent a secret agent year after year to entice him to cross the border back into Mexico. My father was tempted since his one obsession was to return to our homeland.

My mother's interest in her children's affairs was so

great that it reached a poignant, almost comic proportion on one occasion. Not that it seemed anything but sad at the time. In the fall of 1931, with Coach Knute Rockne gone, Notre Dame lost to U.S.C. by a last minute field goal. After hearing the game over the radio, I went looking all over the house for my mother, who had mysteriously disappeared. Finally, I heard some strange noises coming out of a closet. I opened it, and there was my mother, crying her eyes out because of that defeat. Notre Dame was already "ours."

Except for the poverty, the early 1930s were happy years for us. Most of our neighbors were as poor as we were, even though none had such a large family. On one occasion, we were so short of money that my mother took out three or four Mexican coins of solid, heavy silver and asked me to take them to the nearby bank on Sunset Boulevard and see how to much I could get for the silver. I got nothing because the bank was closed by order of President Roosevelt. That was the famous "Bank holiday" that the President used as an emergency to avoid a run on banks.

My contribution to family finances was small, but I remember it with pride. On Sundays, after our large paper route was done, my mother would ask me "¿Cuánto traes?" This meant, "How much have you brought in? I remember earning as much as eight dollars on one weekend and giving that up to pay the gas or the light bills. The earning of a few dollars is not, however, the best memory I have about my years as a newsboy.

Those were the years when I first came in close contact with black people in this country. I only had one black family in my entire paper route, but they were enough to teach me to love them. They were gentle and kind. They were an elderly couple who lived in the poorest house on my entire route. Most houses in that area were brick and white California stucco with tiles. Theirs was a small wooden house with the paint peeling from every wall. They were about midway through my Saturday route of approximately fifty customers. I was usually pretty tired of hauling my heavy wagon up and down those hills before getting to their house. I was especially weary during the hot California summers. Nobody else in those many homes, where they saw me every Saturday and Sunday, ever took any interest in the skinny, brown-skinned newsboy. But that black couple did. They always had something refreshing for me. They would ask me to "set a little while" on one of the wooden rocking chairs they had on their front porch. In the summer, they would then bring me a glass of cool orange juice with ice that they chipped by hand from their old icebox. In the fall and winter, they usually had a cup of hot chocolate or "Ovaltine" for their newsboy. Always, they had a gentle way of showing their love. They had an old victrola on which they played Gospel Music for me to hear. I still love that music of a people with enough joy to sing in the midst of poverty and brutality.

I wonder how my parents were able to help us so much. The four of us older children were good students, usually at the head of our class. Our parents could not read English well, but they managed to encourage us in our homework. I suppose it was really a matter of knowing they were supervising us and willing to help. The trips that my mother made with us to the public libraries certainly helped. Those libraries opened up a whole new world for

us, a world that has never ceased to provoke my curiosity.

My father was involved in some strange activities that my mother never mentioned in detail. I knew that those activities had to do with something going on in Mexico. I didn't understand, of course, what she meant when she said that he was engaged in "politics." All I knew was that it was dangerous. Just how dangerous, I began to realize in 1929 when my father would be absent from the house for many days. He would come back and then be absent again. My mother would gather us in prayer beside her bed. The prayers seemed incredibly long. We spent many hours on our knees praying for my father's safe return. I once asked my mother why we didn't pray for victory—as we did during football games—and she answered that victory was not as important as my father's safety. She explained that there was a new revolution being fought in Mexico and that my father was helping the revolutionaries fight a "wicked government." It turned out that there was religious persecution by the government of Mexico and the people of the central states had taken up arms against a government that had closed up Catholic churches and schools. It was called "la guerra de los Cristeros" (the war of the Christ bearers) and seemed to involve almost every family in four or five central states of Mexico.

At the same time, an opportunist general in one of the northern states bordering on Arizona had also taken up arms against Mexico's central government. Since the President of Mexico was my father's personal enemy, and since my father naturally resented the religious persecution, it was reason enough for him to risk his life in joining the rebellion against that government. He was making trips to an Arizona copper mine where he had a friend who would sell my father large quantities of dynamite. I understood that this friend had been with Pancho Villa during the early days of the Revolution when my father was with Zapata. Zapata and Villa had been friends and, as my mother explained, most revolutionaries admired my father. It was, therefore, natural that they would help him obtain the means to overthrow that government.

All told, my father crossed the Arizona border into Mexico half a dozen times the fall and winter of 1929. And his wife and children did a lot of praying. I now realize why my mother seemed to be always worried and murmuring prayers. That rebellion ended, just as the one my dad started in 1923, because of the U.S. President in Washington deciding to intervene to stop it. This was done by simply placing an embargo on all sales of arms or munitions to the revolutionaries and, at the same time, furnishing munitions, plus airplanes and pilots, to the central government of Mexico. My father returned after the battles of Cananea and Jiménez, towns just south of the Arizona border. He had only been a distributor of dynamite and ideas, but the danger for him was even greater than that of the front-line soldiers. My mother explained that if my father had been captured, the president of Mexico would have ordered his immediate execution. My faith in the power of prayer has been solid ever since those strange days of revolutions.

My father had suffered greatly in seeing the same tyranny remaining in power in Mexico. He wondered when, if ever, his exile was to end. My mother had that same disillusion. But she was also immensely relieved by his safe return. In Mexico, as the wife of a politician with

revolutionary ideas, she had lived with anxiety. Nevertheless, she always insisted that the struggles of a large family in exile had not been bad at all. She preferred being poor and in exile than being the wife of a powerful public figure in peril in his own land.

Those years in Los Angeles were happy ones for me. Even school was good, since I almost always did well in my studies. I learned to type in junior high school, and I was able to save up enough from my paper routes to buy myself a portable typewriter. It took me a year to save up enough, but I did it.

I had discovered model airplanes and they contributed to making those years happy. The thrill of seeing a little airplane, built without any help, running along the ground and then lifting up to fly, is unforgettable. I had to make up my own glue. I did it by mixing thinner from my mother's nail polish and film from photographic negatives—that was my glue. Success in building and flying those little airplanes gave me a sense of achievement. Just as the winning of each merit badge as a Boy Scout made me feel stronger—even without the uniform. It seemed as if everything was going along just fine for me until the day my father came home, leaping with joy and saying, "Se acabó el destierro" ("the exile is over").

That was in the spring of 1933, and it meant the end of what must have been for him an almost unendurable exile.

I am convinced that exile makes love for one's country much deeper than the love of those who have never been forced to live away from their land of birth. The Mexican government had evidently decided that Jorge Prieto Laurens (my dad) no longer had any political base in

Mexico, and it was therefore safe to allow him to return.

On that spring day of 1933, my father was exuberant. In my mother, however, I sensed a strange mixture of joy and fear. I was just a fifteen years old, but I saw a difference in the way my parents reacted that day. She knew that he was a born politician and would return to the same kinds of dangers they had somehow escaped. She had known the wealth that frequently comes with great power, but she had lived the years when political assassinations were common in Mexico. She had as much nostalgia for her country and for her family as my father. But she also had good reasons to fear the political battles that my father so enjoyed.

It took us a full week of rail travel by day and night to reach Mexico City. For us eight children, the trip was full of the wonders of discovery of a new and different land. Our parents made great efforts to point out the beauty of forests, mountains and prairies. In spite of those efforts to show us all that was good, the return to Mexico was a prolonged and frequently painful cultural shock. The shock started right at the border where paved roads in Nogales, Arizona, were replaced by dusty, dirt roads in Nogales, Sonora. The contrast was depressing and unforgettable.

The arrival in Mexico City was a joyful one, with music, flowers and thousands of friends. The political partisans had prepared what seemed to me a triumphant arrival. To this day the memory of that railroad terminal in Mexico City remains a happy memory. Courage and honesty were being rewarded, although Don Jorge's children didn't realize it. Everything seemed strange, including the fact of men embracing men.

The joys of that reception at the terminal turned all

too soon into bewilderment for us children. We went from the occasional fights because of racial bias in Texas and California to a persistent and malicious ridicule in Mexico. This became evident from our very first day in school. Our inability to pronounce Spanish correctly brought down upon us scorn from our classmates. Even some teachers made fun of our "Gringo accent." Our parents had always spoken Spanish to us in the U.S., but we had not learned to write it and we only spoke Spanish at home. All those ten years of speaking only English at school, on the streets, and on the playgrounds naturally left us with an English accent.

We did not understand the ridicule from our own countrymen when we returned in 1933. We knew not the reasons for the resentment most Mexicans seemed to have towards the United States. Even when its historical reasons were explained by our parents, we did not fully understand them. We were, at least for the first few months, Mexicans that could not understand Mexico.

We had to learn what was for us practically a new language. We were learning to read and write for a the second time in our lives. Only this time it was in hostile schools.

Despite our shock, we gradually lost our accent and we became good students. And, we came out stronger for having to fight so many battles. What we had lost in credits we gained in ability to overcome obstacles. I was set back three full years of schooling. In junior high school in Los Angeles, I had almost finished ninth grade. In Mexico City, I was put back into the sixth grade of grammar school. That alone was a severe humiliation. I had almost as many fist fights now, as a Mexican considered a

"Gringo," as I had had in the U.S. where I was considered a "greaser."

In 1934 there were only a few high schools, clubs and the National University with football teams in Mexico. My school only had soccer, and so I decided to show my classmates that the other game was worthwhile. I was able to convince a good number of students that it took more courage to tackle and block than it did to simply kick a round soccer ball. I was persuasive because I truly loved the game.

Our school would not let us into its playgrounds on weekends. So I did what we had done in Los Angeles; I found an empty lot large enough to come close to the size of a regular gridiron. This was not too difficult in the Mexico City of 1934. By the spring of that year, I had already organized two full teams in our neighborhood and we had had some very exciting games.

The problem was the lack of referees to officiate at those games. I always took my rules book with me to games, and I am ashamed to say that I took advantage of my knowledge of English and sometimes interpreted those rules to my team's advantage. When we ran into an opponent that had a very good running back, I took out my book and pointed out something that was not true. I pointed to the rule on the number of allowed incomplete forward passes in one series of downs and told them it meant that the same player could not run with the ball more than twice in the same series of four downs! The opponents could not read that rule book, and I got away with my dishonest interpretation. But only for that game. Soon enough, our opponents found someone else who could read English and I stopped my peculiar interpretation of the rules.

I knew I had been dishonest, but somehow that did not seem so sinful. I was doing it in self-defense since I was the one who usually had to tackle that fast runner from the other team. I was so happy to be playing football again that that sin did not worry me much. Football was even more fun than it had been in California: I was now the only one who knew the intricacies of what is really a rather complicated game. I was player, coach, and referee all at the same time. I had a wonderful feeling of power. It was also the power of knowing two languages.

By the end of 1934 I had caught up and passed my classmates. That Catholic school had the old system of ranking students and giving out a first, second and third place ribbon each Friday. From the middle of the year until the end of the school year, I was consistently the number one student in the entire seventh grade. My pronunciation was still somewhat "Americanized," but I was no longer the subject of ridicule. Life seemed full of promise to me by the end of that school year.

In August of 1935 I contracted rheumatic fever and suffered damage to the valves of my heart. Just as I was beginning to enjoy my country of birth, I became a life-long cardiac patient. Following an attack of strep throat, one morning I woke up with so much pain in my ankles that I could not stand the weight of the bedclothes on them. The next day it was the hips that were painful. So painful was my right hip that I cringed and drew back with pain when a doctor examined the lower right part of my abdomen. By evening my hip and abdomen were much less painful, but I started bleeding from the nose, which is typical of acute rheumatic fever. Shortly thereafter, I had sudden and terrifying congestive heart failure. I had to

overcome one of mankind's great terrors, the experience of asphyxia. I was trying to catch my breath so desperately that my mother could not stand seeing and hearing my despair. She left my room, asking my father to watch over me while she tried to get a doctor. She was unable to find one on that Sunday afternoon and so I had to simply struggle to regain a semblance of normal breathing. My father sat me at a big open bay window, put his chair beside me, and simply said in a firm and very calm voice: "Calma, hijo, esto pasa, esto pasa." (Calm down son, this will pass, this will pass). As he calmly sat down beside me, reading his newspaper, I recalled his reputation of great courage and slowly bought my fear and then my breathing under control.

The next morning a renowned cardiologist came to see me. He made a precise, correct diagnosis and prescribed the correct treatment, but, unfortunately, he brought a medical student with him. This was unfortunate because the student was given what seemed to me a detailed and ominous description of my "condition." Amidst their mysterious medical terminology, I understood that a valve in my heart had been damaged and that the left side of my heart was so inflamed that it "occupied almost the entire left chest" and thus had pushed that lung back to where the student had trouble hearing it.

When I asked the cardiologist about returning to school and about playing football, he was very firm in his answers. He was especially firm in saying that I had to accept the fact that competitive sports were a thing of the past for me.

I had been very fortunate in surviving the acute heart failure of the previous day. I was told that I would need at

least two months of complete bed rest, followed by a careful, gradual return to activity. He did try to encourage me by saying that I could probably return to school "in a few months," but he was very firm in saying no more sports, at all. I recall that those words seemed like a death sentence to me. For many days afterwards, I was about as depressed as a teenager can get. If my mother had not given me *A Tale of Two Cities* and introduced me to the wonders of Charles Dickens, I would have had nothing but morbid thoughts to occupy my mind. As it was, I had to force myself to read that long and sad novel so as to keep my mind off my apparently dismal future.

The treatment that was prescribed was very intense. They literally filled me up with salicylates to put out the fire that rheumatic fever actually is. Both the salicylates and the good nursing that forced me to eat were to work a near miracle. But meanwhile, I was as down as down could be. I did, however, receive more tender loving care than the average patient. Much more. My mother cared for me with a gentle intensity that literally pulled me up out of that bed and, eventually, to the playing fields of Mexico City.

But first I had to live through two long months of lying in bed, feverish and depressed, wondering too much about my future. Ovaltine came back into my life as did a British concoction called Bovril that looked like dark honey and tasted like salty broth. My mother gave it to me with assurances that it would "build up my blood"—and of course my strength. I was given every food I craved. The food made a "cushion" that would protect my stomach lining so it could tolerate the large doses of salicylates.

My convalescence was only complicated when, a

month into my illness, my sister Socorro and my brother Pedro both came down with typhoid fever. They were put in the same room with me so that we could be more easily cared for. My mother was young and healthy, but she had a tremendous burden in caring for three seriously ill children at the same time.

Just before my illness, my parents had bought me a new American football. It was the first leather football I had ever had, and it sat there on top of a clothes closet where I could only see it and wonder if I would ever get to use it. In my good days, when the fever subsided somewhat, I could see myself throwing long passes and returning punts all the way for touchdowns. When the fever was high my spirits were low, and I wondered if that cardiologist had perhaps been right in his prognosis.

My mother reminded me that my doctor was a world famous physician and that the next time he saw me my heart would have probably healed almost completely. She also added cream of wheat to my food diet and Sor Juana Inez de la Cruz to my literary diet.

The second cardiologist found me much improved and suggested that I return to school "in a few months." But he too said competitive sports were a thing of the past for me. A sedentary life is difficult for most youngsters, and it was very difficult for me. In spite of the great literature by Charles Dickens and Sor Juana Inez de la Cruz that my mother had furnished, I felt an irresistible need to get outdoors. If I could not run, as the doctors had said, I could at least feel the sun and the wind in my face. I convinced my brother Carlos to come out with me after his school hours and play "touch" football in the nearby empty meadows. Mexico City in 1936 still had large empty spaces and

I felt free crossing them during these improvised games. We took my new football and went out to throw passes, to kick spiral punts, and, above all, to feel free. I didn't run, but I could play the deep man in punt formation and from there I could scramble away from onrushing linemen with feints and long strides. Just the feel of that football in my hands was a joy. I became a better passer since I was not allowed to run. I learned to evade onrushing linemen and, best of all, I unknowingly rehabilitated my heart with that early exercise. It was limited exercise, but exercise nonetheless.

However, those games were infrequent because it was difficult to get enough friends to come out after school. I didn't have school homework, but they did. High schools in Mexico during those years gave out a great deal of homework. English was becoming increasingly required and most schools required their students to learn French. Three languages, plus the constantly increasing amount of science being required, made for a good deal of study.

Except for those rare moments of joy throwing and kicking that football, my life was empty. I had too much time to dwell on my illness and on my apparently limited future. Laboring under the belief that I was destined to a lifetime of disability, I became very depressed. I tried prayer; my God, did I try prayer! I wandered in and out of countless churches. In my neighborhood and far from it, I went into every church I could find, praying for health. With the urgency of youth, I pleaded for a return to a normal life.

In that desperate search for normality, I was taken to see many doctors. They all listened to my clinical history and examined me for the heart-valve damage. And they all said, "No school yet." For more than a year I went in and out of churches and doctor's offices with no sense of improvement. Since I couldn't go back to school, I was also cut off for the better part of each day from all friends. It was little wonder that after a year and a half of such a sick role, I was truly despondent.

On several occasions in 1936, I seriously considered suicide. I came within a few feet of jumping off a high cliff on the Avenida Insurgentes. But somehow faith and the desire to continue living prevailed, and I was able to discard those horrible thoughts.

During that first year and a half of my illness, my troubles were compounded by unnecessary surgery. It was believed that rheumatism and arthritis were caused, or aggravated by, abscessed teeth or infected tonsils. As in most widespread beliefs, there is sometimes a kernel of truth to be found in them. In the case of rheumatic fever, it was known that there is indeed a relationship between streptococcal throat infection and subsequent rheumatic fever with its cardiac complications. It was also well documented that large numbers of young people living in close quarters, such as boarding schools and in military camps, often developed rheumatic fever. I was living in a small house with seven brothers and sisters. And I obviously had a defective immune system. At the time, tonsillectomies were being done on many children who had throat infections more than once in one winter. It was also being done to prevent rheumatic fever. This had never been proven to be an effective method of preventing this illness, but it was a widespread practice nevertheless.

One year after the damage to my heart, and therefore utterly useless as a preventive measure, two physicians decided to do a tonsillectomy on me. A pediatrician and an ear-nose-and-throat specialist took a terrified sixteen-year old boy and sat him down in a dental chair, which made the operation much more dangerous. I didn't realize the danger, of course, I only feared the very thought of an operation. My mother knew that I was going to have a terrifying ordeal and prepared me for it. The night before the operation, she gave me a convincing lecture on the need to tolerate pain, explaining how women generally go through much more physical pain than men. She used the example of childbirth, of course, but she also told me that women suffer much more because of man's indifference, brutality, and exploitation.

What was intended as a lesson about courage became an unforgettable view of life. That same afternoon, she also gave me a copy of the classic poem by Sor Juana Inez de la Cruz on "Hombres Necios" (Foolish Men). She not only prepared me to face that dreadful operation, she gave me a viewpoint on how to treat women, a viewpoint that has served me well all my life.

Thus prepared, I was at least determined to be brave. I was not prepared, however, for the horrors of a tonsillectomy under local anesthesia. After strapping my arms down to that dental chair, they put a metal bit between my upper and lower teeth. It looked like the ones they use on horses, and I felt trapped. The throat specialist then proceeded to bring out a huge glass syringe with a terribly long needle that looked thick as a nail to me. He stuck that needle deep into the back of my throat, waited a few minutes for the anesthesia to take effect, and started to cut away at my tonsils. Since there is no way that four hands can fit in a child's throat simultaneously, the pediatrician

did nothing during the entire operation but stand next to me, telling me not to move and that all was going well. All during the operation I could feel and hear the suction tube pulsing away under my tongue. Twice it stopped working and I had to spit out what seemed to me to be rivers of bright red blood. The second time, I almost panicked, but my mother's words came back to me and brought a measure of calm. I said some very fervent prayers and made some very solemn promises to God. I promised that I would never knowingly hurt a woman. I was not bargaining with God, since there was no way I could avoid or stop the suffering I was going through, but I felt I was making promises that were binding and that God would consider them when judging me.

That operation did not improve my health. All it did was improve my spiritual outlook on suffering. And, it also contributed to my state of depression. I was put back into the role of patient, a patient who had lost a good amount of blood and suffered more than any adolescent should be made to suffer. The lesson of all the terrors I went through that day served me well when I eventually became a physician.

My mother, of course, noticed my continued and deepening depression and decided to do something drastic to change my attitude. My father had a brother living in the capital of the state of San Luis Potosi. This was the state where my father had been governor and he still had many friends there. It was also the only state where Catholic schools were open in the Mexico of 1936. A sojourn in San Luis Potusi seemed just right for a young man with a "damaged heart." Mexico City is on a plateau more than three thousand meters above sea level and is

considered too much of a strain for most cardiac patients. San Luis was promising. It was with high hopes that my mother and I took the overnight train to San Luis.

We arrived at about sundown and I was impressed by the fact that there was hardly a soul out walking, either downtown or in the neighborhoods we traversed. It was eerie to see such deserted streets. I could almost hear the silence. Everything but the movie houses was closed down, and it was still early in the evening. The silence and solitude of those streets seemed somehow ominous. It certainly appeared to be a sad place to live in, even temporarily.

My uncle was very wealthy, but his house was very cold. He and my aunt had never had children and, naturally, didn't know much about how to deal with a teenage boy much less how to motivate a youngster struggling with chronic illness. Their rather cold greeting—my uncle was just recovering from a long siege of typhoid fever—and the very hard bed they assigned me were a poor start for all of us. To top off the sad welcome, that house was poorly lighted; my uncle did not like to waste electricity.

My mother did her best to convince me that it would all work out for my recovery—which it eventually and almost miraculously did—but that first night was so depressing. She stayed for a few days, trying to encourage me all the while. We visited some distant relatives with twelve daughters and one son. It was a weird experience sitting in a large living room surrounded by some fifteen people all perched on nineteenth-century sofas and chairs. Some of those daughters were middle-aged spinsters, but at least two were pretty young girls. These two awakened some hidden sense of happiness in me, although it was clear we had very little in common. The life of a provincial

family in San Luis early in this century was very different from the life of Mexicans that had lived ten years in the United States, survived a revolution, a depression, and a deportation. We might as well have been visitors from Mars.

After I had become acquainted with these distant cousins and I had seen the city—which was easy to cover in less than two days—I was taken to the local Catholic High School. There I found out the harm that unreasonable fears can do. The "Brother" in charge of that school rejected my application with hardly a glance at my school record. He rejected me as soon as he heard my medical history, saying that he "did not want to be responsible for having a 'cardiac' running back and forth on his playgrounds."

Thus unable to attend school while living in a city where only a handful of people even knew of my existence, I had nowhere to find friends. I became extremely lonely. I did find a copy of an American magazine called *Boy's Life*. In it I found directions for making a model airplane. My uncle was willing to give me enough money to send for a balsa wood, glue and rubber strips. Building and flying those little rubber-powered airplanes was like a joyful return to my happy years in Los Angeles and helped me retain my sanity.

I was still wandering into every church I could find, always pleading for a return to health and to a normal life. As happens with so many that are afflicted with chronic diseases, I wanted the miracle of a sudden return to health. It was during those lonely days in San Luis that I first doubted the existence of God. That, of course, made me feel guilty and increased my depression. I stumbled and

struggled in my solitude. The special emptiness that only a teenager knows had me in it's grip.

It was only natural that I practically stopped eating and started suffering from insomnia, which is frequently found in those that can't or won't exercise. The insomnia was made worse by my vivid imagination and my fear of permanent disability. By the time my aunt and uncle decided to call my mother from Mexico City to come for me, I was all skin and bones.

Mothers can work miracles with wayward or sick children, and my mother did just that. She came and started me on a whole program of enthusiastic recovery. At first the enthusiasm was all hers, but it soon infected me. She filled me up with tomato juice that she prepared herself, telling me how the extra lemon juice that she added would give me vitamin C and give me all kinds of protection and strength. Then she helped me with my model airplanes. One morning she took me to one little shop after another until she found some pins with large round beads for heads. She gave these to me and said that I could now pin the balsa wood down to the airplane blue prints more securely and without hurting my fingers. The way she had patiently looked into store after store until she found those pins made me realize how much she loved me. From those simple everyday episodes she went on to the more difficult task of finding a way to challenge me to want to return to enjoying life.

On the third or fourth day of her stay in San Luis, my mother took me walking all the way to the central plaza in town. The governor's palace overlooks that plaza and, therefore, the site had a special significance for both of us. She sat me down on a bench facing that building where

my father had once been governor. She did not need to make any references to my father's courage, nor did she do so. She simply said, "I don't believe that you are as sick as those cardiologists have said you were. They examined you many months ago, when the fever was raging. But young people heal fast. There is a doctor here that is your father's friend. He is widely renowned as the best physician in San Luis, and he owes your father a favor. I want to take you to see him, but it's only worthwhile if you have a strong desire to live a normal life. Don't you want to play football again? I noticed that you have taken down your Notre Dame banner from the wall next to your bed. Have you given up, or are you still willing to come back to school in Mexico City and play quarterback with a regular school team?"

Those may not have been the exact words she used that morning, but they were certainly the essence of her challenge. I don't remember exactly how I answered. I was tired of seeing doctors, but I felt I could not ignore her reasoning nor her love for me.

That day, the journey back to normal life began for me. From the square we walked to that famous doctor's office. Everything in downtown San Luis was close by in those days. On the way she explained to me how this doctor, Jesús N. Noyola, had been able to do postgraduate studies in Paris, France, studies that helped make him such an outstanding physician. When my father was govenor, he had befriended the doctor. He had convinced the Secretary of Education—by phone to Mexico City and with that young medical student in the governor's office—to concede a full scholarship stipend, with living expenses included, so that the young student could study for at least two years in France. That governor was very powerful at the time since he was also President of the National Congress. That young and ambitious medical student had nobody to recommend him to the equally young governor. He simply showed the governor his medical school record and asked for his help. That was not the usual way people obtained favors from politicians in Mexico, but both my father and the student were willing to do the unorthodox.

The memory of that visit is one of the most cherished recollections of my long life. Every detail of that day seems fresh in my memory. Even the way Dr. Noyola entered his office was pleasant and attractive. He had a series of examining and treatment rooms surrounding a colorful patio. The patio was full of flowers and large potted plants. On the red brick pathways surrounding that patio he had large comfortable chairs where his patients waited endlessly. It did not seem like a doctor's waiting room at all. He came in crossing diagonally through the patio, waving his arms to both sides and joking about his being late. He had an exuberant optimism that was contagious.

I immediately found out that he was a careful, consummate clinician. The way in which he listened to my medical history and did his physical examination is forever engraved in my mind. He was slow and thorough, but above all he was gentle. As he put away his stethoscope, Dr. Noyola said exactly what I needed to hear. "You do have a heart murmur, but it is not of the serious type of valve damage. More than anything else, you are frightened to death. From the way you describe your illness, I can see that you are literally swimming in self-pity. You seem to see yourself as a permanent invalid."

"Well, the other doctors all said . . ."

"I think I know what those cardiologists must have told you, but that was at the height of your rheumatic fever. In any case, I know perhaps a little more about rheumatic heart disease than they do."

"Why?"

"Because my only son died from cardiac complications of rheumatic fever, and your heart is nowhere as damaged as his was."

Those words, and his examination, brought me back to the land of the living. They brought back my hopes, my dreams.

Dr. Noyola did not content himself with that reassurance. He proceeded to ask me if I liked tennis. Telling him that I did, but that I preferred football, made him laugh. He said that they didn't have that "crazy" sport in San Luis but that they had good tennis courts, and he invited (actually ordered) me to his club for that weekend. He said that we were going to "play a few sets together." In a matter-of-fact way he was giving me the chance to see for myself if I was really an invalid. As we were leaving, he put his hand on my shoulder and said, "Damn it, son, put on your father's hat." By that reference to my father's legendary courage, he was, in fact, ordering me to be courageous.

And so, with lingering fears mixed with curiosity and hope, I went to his private tennis club the following Saturday afternoon. I was able to play several sets of rather fast tennis without once falling short of breath. My heart had recovered!

The years of disability ended that week. The nights of insomnia also disappeared. I continued to play tennis with Dr. Noyola for several Saturdays, whenever he did not

have an emergency or a delivery for one of his obstetrical patients. He also had me come to his office twice a week for "liver shots." I realize now that he was being more than my doctor, he was acting as a surrogate father for the months I spent waiting for the next school term to start in Mexico City.

Early in 1937 I was back home and enrolled in a school (the Technologic Institute) that had heavy shop work as part of its curriculum. It also had good football teams. American football teams. The Tech was a large public school that included junior high school, senior high school, and college all on the same campus. It was so large that they did not do physical examinations on entering students. So nobody there ever had a record of my rheumatic heart disease.

Once admitted, I started to build up my strength with calisthenic exercises. I was five feet, nine inches tall and weighed only sixty kilos (about 130 lbs.). Most of the students I was going to play with and against were bigger and heavier than I was. Every morning I would get up before sunrise and go up on the roof of our house and do very energetic exercises. This gave me, as a bonus, a very unique experience. I was able to see some of nature's awesome beauty. In the late 1930s, the air over Mexico City was clean, with a transparency and luminosity that was everyone's delight, especially artists. As I jumped up and down doing my exercises, I would see the sun rising between the two mighty volcanoes that overlook the city from the east. At first, a faint orange light would appear at the top of the two volcanoes. Then that light reached all of Ixtaccihuatl, the volcano to the north, and then it quickly illuminated all of Popocateptl, to the south. As I watched

fascinated, the pulsing luminosity extended quickly downward from those peaks until it filled the entire valley and city. I stood there in wonder and delight at so much beauty.

History has it that the Aztec nation worshiped the sun. Those mornings, I understood why the Aztecs must have thought that sunrise was a miracle of their gods. I have seen many sunrises and many sunsets in Canada, the U.S., and in Mexico, but none to surpass the silent beauty of those faraway dawns. It was pure joy to be able to see how those days started, to feel strong with the sun on my face, and to be able to go to classes, to labs, and to shop-work.

One of the early morning classes was Blacksmith Shop and nobody struck those anvils with more vigor and pleasure than that born-again student. Those shops were my delight in my first year back in school. But they were not the only good things at my new school. There were at least two very good and memorable professors. One was the professor of Geometry and the other taught a course called *Anatomy, Physiology and Hygiene*. It was generally considered by my classmates as a relatively unimportant course. Since our junior high school was fundamentally a trade school, that attitude was understandable. Even the elderly physician who gave the course seemed strangely out of place in school that was basically for crafts and trades. Nevertheless, he was a true teacher and I will always remember him. His name was Dr. José Silva and what is most memorable to me is his lecture on alcoholism. He first described the biochemistry of what happened to the livers, brains, and nerve endings of alcoholics. Then he spoke of the reasons why we should never judge such people harshly. Amongst other reasons, he reminded us that we would probably never understand the depths of despair and failure nor the loneliness of an alcoholic, and thus we would have no basis for passing judgment on those suffering from alcoholism. It was not a lecture on the sciences of Anatomy and Physiology. It was a lecture on compassion. It was, perhaps, the best lecture I ever heard in my many years as a student in Mexico and the United States. I have since attended many conferences on the subject in both countries. I have also read extensively on the subject. But nothing I have heard or read impressed me as deeply as that lecture by my professor at the Instituto Tecnico Industrial in 1938.

As soon as the football tryouts for the 1938 junior high team were announced, I came out to that little stadium and applied for the position of quarterback. I was told by members of the previous year's team that I had very little chance of winning that position. This seemed ridiculous since they all admitted that the reigning quarterback was not very good. But, the coach was his brother. I watched that young man throw passes and was convinced I could beat him out. He actually had very little ability and he knew next to nothing about strategy.

During my sick years I had read just about everything there was to read about the game of football. I knew the football philosophy of Amos Alonzo Stagg of Chicago, as well as that of Knute Rockne, of course. I had even read a little book by Frank Carideo (Rockne's last and perhaps best quarterback), entitled *Kicking the American Football.* I had read something about the double wing-back formation by Coach Pop Warner of Stanford, as well as the book *Practical Football* by Fritz Krisller of Michigan.

I knew the strengths and the weaknesses of every

type of offense and defense. I had knowledge that my future teammates couldn't have because they didn't read English. Above all, I had a strong determination to fulfill the challenge my mother had made to me in San Luis. I was determined to become, eventually, the best quarterback in town.

That first tryout in the spring of 1938 was a great victory for me. I could pass, kick and run the ball much better than the other contenders, including the coach's brother. At the end of that session they passed out the new jerseys to the 22 finalists, the ones that would make up the first and second teams for the school. I was as happy as a boy with a new bicycle when they gave me my new jersey, some battered shoulder and kidney pads, and an old helmet, all handed down from our high school team.

Our team was using the old Stanford double wingback formation plus a few plays from punt formation. Most of the other teams in the league used the Notre Dame shift into a single wingback box. That was the type of formations and plays that had prevailed in the U. S. for the previous fifteen or twenty years.

There was very little passing being done in Mexico at the time. For that matter, they were not yet doing much passing in the U.S. either. The only innovation in the mid-1930's seemed to be the increased use of lateral passing. The great passers that revolutionized the game were just coming onto the gridirons up north. Sammy Baugh and Davey O'Brien of Texas, Sid Luckman of Columbia, and Frankie Albert of Stanford came on the scene between 1938 and 1940. The T-formation also appeared on the playing fields of America and changed the game to a faster, more exciting contest.

The Quarterback Who Almost Wasn't

Cornell University was using the lateral pass with great success, but it seemed as if nobody except "Chili Beans" cared to use it in Mexico. The rules limited the passing game with penalties of five yards for the throwing of more than one incomplete pass in the same series of downs. They further limited passing by requiring that the passer be at least five yards behind the line of scrimmage when throwing a forward pass.

Those rules were changed in 1938 or 39, just in time for me as it turned out. I came into organized football at just the right time. With my love for those long arching spiral flights of football, I could not have been happier than I was those first days as the starting quarterback for my school.

It seemed as if I was dreaming when we lined up for our first game in 1938. It was in a little stadium that seated only five thousand spectators and had never been known to be filled to capacity. That game was against a team called University Extension, a rather weird name for a junior high school. My father explained that it was founded as a political ploy, simply intended to downgrade the importance of our working-class school.

As we lined up for the kickoff, I was surprised to see that the opponents had a veritable giant among their players. We were only a junior high school and that player was 6 feet 4 inches tall. But he was very clumsy and turned out to be a ringer recruited to intimidate us and not because of his athletic ability.

As we lined up for the start of that game, I remembered my first game on the sandlots in Los Angeles. I remembered that "Chili Beans" could run, tackle and pass with players bigger and stronger than he was, and he could

do it quite well.

That first game was like so many games where a team is so inexperienced that the players seem to get in each other's way. Nobody came even close to the opponent's goal, and we played a boring zero-to-zero tie. My mother was one of the dozen or so spectators. That was the first Saturday afternoon of the many she was to witness her son playing. She naturally tried to cheer me up after that game, saying it was to be expected that we played poorly since we hardly knew our plays. She always understood how complicated football is and that encouraged me greatly.

We had two weeks for preparation before our second game and we used them to good advantage. Reluctantly, our coach asked me to bring my "Gringo" books and I brought "Practical Football" by Fritz Krissler.

From that book we took half a dozen pass plays and put them into our playbook. The new passing attack, well practiced, and the two lonely years spent in those meadows scrambling away from onrushing opponents, paid off immediately. I could complete passes with accuracy up to a distance of forty yards. We were in a junior high league, but I was on the average two years older than my teammates and my opponents. They had not lost two years of schooling as I had, but they also did not know much about pain and about football, as I did.

Most important was the fact that they did not seem to have the fierce determination to be a good player that I certainly had. I enjoyed even our practice scrimmages, practice sessions that my teammates found generally tedious. I made them interesting by throwing pass after pass after pass. I also practiced the "quick kick" in which

the quarterback (usually not the regular kicker or punter), standing only three or four yards behind and to one side of the center, takes the throw from center and kicks it on the first, second or third down. This relinquishes control of the football, but it almost always takes the opponents by surprise since kicking is ordinarily reserved for the fourth or last down. I did this in several games to set the enemy far back near their own goal line.

Because I was the quarterback, I had to call out the numbers as we lined up for each play. Early on in that season, my left halfback, Roberto Suárez, noticed my yankee accent. He started calling me "Pocho." That is a pejorative name tag used in Mexico to identify those of Mexican descent born in the U.S., or Mexicans that had lived in the U.S. and liked the country. My father did not like the new nickname in the sports pages, but just as "Chili Beans" had stuck to me in California, "Pocho" followed me during my five seasons as student and player in Mexico City. A few of my teammates disliked a United States they only knew from the movies, but I quickly won their respect by playing better than any other quarterback. I took great delight in breaking tackles on punt returns, and some of the biggest players on our team found ways to evade having to tackle me in practice sessions.

Our second game of that season was against a senior high school and we played an amazingly good game. With only two weeks of practice with the new plays, I was able to complete four passes for touchdowns and another half-dozen for shorter gains. On the first series of downs, I threw a pass for thirty yards and a touchdown. On our second possession, I called for a short forward pass to our right end, followed by three lateral passes. We scored with that series too. A sportswriter wrote that these plays "flowed like poetry" and that we looked as good as any college team in their execution. From that day on my reputation as a good quarterback seemed made. All quarterbacks called their own plays with no help from coaches or observers on the sidelines, and that really tested quarterbacks under pressure. I enjoyed the challenge immensely. I knew full well, even in those early days of my sports career, that news reporters contribute to the "mystique" that surrounds and follows successful quarterbacks.

My two brothers, Guillermo (two years younger than I) and Carlos (three and a half years younger), knew the game almost as well as I did. But they played it simply for the fun of it and not with any passion. Carlos did establish a record for consecutive completed passes (16 in one single game in 1941), but he played just for the fun of it and missed practice frequently. Guillermo, the older of my three brothers, always cared more about his studies and grades. Successful in academics, he put relatively small effort into the game. Our youngest brother, Pedro, did not play until 1945, and then only two seasons of high school ball. He was 6 feet 3 inches tall and was a spectacular pass receiver. But he also had no real passion for the game and left it after a sensational victory in 1945. He played left end on offense and defense; he also called his team's plays instead of the quarterback. He caught something like a dozen passes that last game of his.

I played with a burning determination to be the best quarterback in each of the three leagues I played in. My mother was in the stands watching her ex-cardiac son for almost every game of my five seasons of play. Watching me win almost all those games must have been a wonder, a

special joy for her. Those were glorious afternoons for both of us.

There is a Mexican song that tells about "la manana jovial de mi vida" (that happy morning of my life). That is what those years from 1938 to 1941 actually were for me. If ever a sport had great value for a player, football had it for me. It inspired me to want to do well in whatever I attempted and helped me become a good student and not just a good quarterback.

That first year back in school was a year of continuous and pleasant discoveries. I quickly found out that the bus I had to take from school and back home passed by a private school for girls. It didn't matter to me that I was in a trade school and wearing workingmen's overalls. Private schools in Mexico were almost exclusively for the affluent, but I didn't give class distinctions a second thought. Every one of those girls seemed pretty to me and I tried to date more than one. I was a very self-assured quarterback, but socially I had no idea how to approach a girl. I was never successful in dating any of those rich girls, but it was fun just trying. It made me feel full of life to see them get on that bus and fill it with their laughter and their voices.

After our first victory, the team did arrange for an afternoon dance that started what I believed would be my first romance. The problem was that the first girl I dated after that dance was not the least bit interested in football nor in microscopes nor in science. We had nothing in common. She even disliked Cole Porter's music! I would wait at the corner of her house for endless hours trying to have a few moments to talk to her, but to little avail. The second time we met, it was at a chaperoned dance. Almost all young girls in Mexico had to have chaperons in those days. I only danced twice with her. The reason for not dancing more was that, on the second time around, she asked me if I danced every piece as a waltz! I finally gave up on that attempt at romance. She didn't seem to realize that I was a "great" quarterback! The newspapers did, but she didn't. With great sadness, I gave up on her and returned to my schoolwork and my football. I recognized the wisdom in my uncle (also my math tutor) when he called me to his house and explained that I was simply in love with the idea of being in love.

Once I got over my attempt at romance, my schoolwork naturally improved. And so did my football. The team was increasingly convinced that I could lead them to victory. More than most sports, football requires leadership on the field. Once a quarterback proves he is an accurate passer and that he knows not only strategy but also when to change it, confidence builds up and victory becomes the norm. That was exactly what happened with our teams from the Instituto Politécnico Nacional (the school's new name as of 1939) during the years 1938 to 1941.

It was exciting to be in that school as it was coming onto the national scene. Our team helped with some rather sensational headlines. In five seasons, we lost only three games, tied two, and won all the rest. After our second game in 1938, I knew that my team trusted me. They had reason to because of my three touchdown passes and that short pass with the three laterals taking us all the way to the goal. I sensed their trust and realized that sports writers, with their exuberant praise, contributed substantially to my success. Nevertheless, all through those five seasons, I went on the field with the nagging worry about my

"damaged" heart. That worry was nothing more than just that since I had the evidence that I could run back and forth as well as any of my teammates. By my third season that worry was almost entirely forgotten. I knew English and had studied football tactics and strategy extensively. That was fulfillment enough for me. At least for the time being.

It would have been easy to assume an air of superiority based on this and on my initial victories. Fortunately for me, I recognized good advice when it was offered. One day I was at practice with my junior high school team and noticed that the coach of our senior high and college teams was in the stands near our side of the field. This was after four consecutive victories and I was feeling rather important. I was trying to show the head coach how much in command I was by shouting stridently at my team. Our coach called for time-out and told me that the head coach was in the stands and wanted to talk to me. With some trepidation I went up to meet Coach Salvador Mendiola. He was a small very serene person. He had once been a great lineman and had a good reputation in every way. He had not yet won a national championship but was highly respected.

The lesson he gave me that day was probably the main reason I went on to become a good quarterback. In a very quiet manner, he told me that I was "a pretty good passer, and should make a really good one if I practiced enough." Then he asked what seemed to me a strange question. He asked me if I wanted to become a truly great quarterback? I must have given the obvious answer, but what I remember is his advice. He told me that if I wanted to be the best leader, I would have to earn more than just the respect of my teammates. He said it would be necessary that they "like you as a person. You are not going to win too many games if your team doesn't really like you. Remember that this is not the army, where you have to follow orders. It is a game and you and your teammates are supposed to enjoy it."

I went back to our practice, knowing that I had received good advice. From that day on I tried to follow it, and we did enjoy our games and even some of our practice scrimmages. Those few words from a wise teacher were the reason behind three championships and many great, almost incredible victories. I played under coach Mendiola for two high school and two college seasons, and had a wonderful time in the process.

During my first season of junior high school football I thought my main task was that of building up physical strength to take the pounding of such a game. I did more calisthenics than any of my teammates and very seldom missed practice. When I did miss, it was usually because of school work. The two years out of school had taken their toll. I did not have good study habits and I had lost most of my ability to understand mathematics. Success in football was fine, and both my mother and I rejoiced in it. But she also insisted in telling me that my father would demand good grades in every subject at the end of the year. That was his condition to allow me to continue what he considered a brutal game.

By the time I ended my first season of playing football, my younger brother Guillermo was two years ahead of me in schooling and leading his class. My sister, a year younger than I, was at the head of her whole school. So I had to make an extra effort, not so much because of sibling rivalries, but because I needed good grades to be allowed by my father to continue playing. I needed the knowledge too, and desperately wanted to learn science. I still wanted to go to the University of Notre Dame in the United States someday. Given the modest economic conditions of our family, this last was apparently an impossible dream. Impossible perhaps, but never abandoned.

To my great good fortune, I found an excellent tutor in mathematics. An uncle on my mother's side was a retired civil engineer and he offered to help me with my struggles in math. He enjoyed teaching and taught me more than mathematics. He taught me the importance of orderly thinking and the need for discipline. He started out with geometry and gradually got me to understand advanced mathematics. By the time we reached differential calculus, I was in love with mathematics. It was an even greater achievement than all those touchdown passes since I had no natural talent for the subject. It was the discipline of hard work. It was also more important than any sports victory, although I naturally did not realize it at the time.

That first year back in the normal "land of the living," as my mother called it, was full of wonders. We won the public school championship and then defeated the private club champions.

That citywide championship was the first one ever played in Mexico and it was decided in a game between us and the team that had won the championship between private club teams. The affluent families in Mexico, just as the rich in most countries, had their private clubs with all kinds of modern facilities such as swimming pools, tennis courts, trainers and coaches. They usually had good athletes, too. Perhaps good nutrition and good coaching were advantages they generally enjoyed. I played against that team five times in three different leagues, and we won three of those five encounters.

The game for the city championship in 1938 was played in the rain. The rain which had started out as an ordinary shower became a driving storm by the middle of the game. Football played in the rain usually favors the team with a strong running attack. Our opponents, the "Wachachara" club, had a strong running game whereas our strength was in passing. They were the favored team and should have won. It is very difficult to throw a wet and muddy football, but I did it successfully that afternoon. I did it by calling passes early in the game, before the field became a soggy morass of mud. It was one of my better games of that year. By half-time, when the rain became a storm, we were ahead 7 to 0 and had been able to contain their running back. He was a great runner, destined to win the 100 and 200 meter dashes in the next year's Pan-American Games. After the half, it became almost impossible to pass and harder to catch up with Julián Amezcua, their great running back. He scored around end in the third quarter.

With the score tied and only about five minutes to play, I was able to save the day and take my team to victory. They punted the ball and it landed in the mud like a dead duck on our two-yard line. That meant we would have to punt out from deep in our own end zone just to keep them from gaining possession of the ball near our goal line. In the huddle I called for a punt. Roberto Suárez was our punter, and he was a good punter. But he was also very independent and stubborn. He refused, point blank, to punt us out of danger. I called time-out to find out the rea-

son for this unusual refusal to follow his quarterback's orders. He said that handling the pass from center and trying to kick that muddy and slippery football made a fumble not only possible but likely. Since a fumble in the end-zone would certainly lose us the game, he did not want to be responsible for losing the championship. He was stubborn and reminded me that I frequently stayed on after practice sessions to punt with him. So he said, "Why don't you punt us out of here?" I was angry and a time-out is only two minutes long, so there was no time and no use to argue. We lined up in punt formation and I took the pass from center, deep in my end-zone. I tried to remember all of Frank Carideo's advice in his book about kicking, and I turned out to be a good student. God only knows how I was able to do it, but I got off a nearly perfect kick and that heavy wet ball went in a high and long spiral all the way past mid-field and landed on their 35-yard line. A 65-yard punt in the rain and with a muddy football! That was the best punt of the year and the best I ever made. It saved the day because it took us out of danger and placed our opponents very far from our goal and on a muddy field. It was so muddy by then that even Amezcua had a hard time even keeping his footing. They became demoralized while we became jubilant over the results of that kick. A few plays later, one of their backs fumbled on their 40-yard line and we proceeded to smash our way down to their goal line. We scored by doing the opposite of what we had done all season. Since the first game we had been successful with a spin play in which I would fake a handoff to our fullback who would go smashing into the center of the line while I waited a couple of seconds and completed the spin, running the ball myself off their defensive left guard. The

threat of our fullback running into the center of the line usually drew our opponent's left guard in, leaving a hole between guard and tackle through which I was able to run for good gains all season long. This time, with less than a minute to play and with the ball in our possession on their one-yard line, I spun around and actually left the ball in my fullback's hands while I completed the spin as if I still had the ball. Their defensive linemen followed me and left a hole through which our fullback ran into the end zone for the winning touchdown.

That made us the city champions and almost assured me of the starting quarterback position for our high school team after graduation from junior-high.

Senior high school in Mexico at that time was only three years long. Those high school years are the time when students normally decide their vocation. I was no exception to that crucial decision making, only I agonized perhaps more than the average. I was in an engineering course because I had done so well in math. But I was in love with microscopes. As I entered high school and saw more and more science, I became increasingly inclined to change to a biology track. I had a vague hope of someday becoming a physician, a doctor of medicine. But I was still not sure that my health would be up to the stress of medical school. What a strange worry for a quarterback that had just led his team to school and citywide championships!

Everybody that I knew spoke of medical school as if were an ominous and very difficult task. It turned out that this pessimistic outlook came from the failure of an uncle who had been the only one on either my paternal or maternal side of the family to ever attempt medical school. The lingering and not very reasonable worries about my "damaged" heart also had something to do with my dilemma.

In 1940 I was twenty-one years old and having such a good time at football and studying that I did not spend too much time in agonizing about my vocation. I was more interested in finding some beautiful girl to fall in love with the great quarterback I thought I was. Those were the years of romantic dreams. Mexican music contributed much to my romanticism. Even though I failed miserably in the matter of dating girls, I enjoyed the music, the colors, and the many pretty girls that seemed to be everywhere. It was as if I were discovering Mexico and its beauty all over again.

Automobiles and money did not even enter into my dreams of those years. There was no reason for me to expect either of those two things and, therefore, they did not seem important. Their lack was hardly noticeable to me. It was good just to be young and enjoying my victory over illness. The lack of material things, such as an automobile, was no distress at all. I felt surrounded by so much that was interesting and so much that was beautiful that I even enjoyed school.

Our junior high school team passed almost intact to become the starting team for the new high school of the Instituto Politécnico Nacional of 1939. With that team came Juan José Salas, one of the best pass receivers of all time in Mexico. He ran with great speed and could jump higher to bring down a pass than anyone I have ever known. He literally pulled passes down out of the sky on many occasions. I purposely threw them high because Knute Rockne had so advised in one of his books in writing about long passes where you have to lead your receiver.

Juan José Salas could usually reach them. We became good friends after that second game of our first season together in 1938. We had extra practices together, and I felt that we were just like Gus Dorais and Knute Rockne had been when they practiced those summers on the sand dunes of northern Indiana. At least we confirmed what Dorais and Rockne had proved, namely that determination and practice lead to great victories.

For the five seasons that Salas and I played together we completed passes for touchdowns in almost every game. The opponents saw us using the same pass patterns year after year and yet were unable to stop us.

Our opponents must have known that, in a pinch, when we seemed stopped in our tracks, I would throw the same long crossover pass. It was a play taken from the book *Practical Football*, and not too difficult for an opponent to figure out. The two halfbacks would run straight down for about ten yards and then cut sharply to the outside while the two ends would run fifteen yards straight down and then cross over in an arch to the opposite side. Perhaps one reason they were never able to break it up was that I frequently threw to one of the halfbacks or to the other end.

Of course, I occasionally threw off the mark for an incomplete pass, and I was intercepted four times in five seasons of play. But in the critical moments of all our important games, I was able to complete "number #90," as that pass was labeled. Even the way I called it in the huddle seemed to cause the team to respond with confidence. I found out at a party in one of our opponent's home that the "Universitarios" (as we called those connected in any way with the National University) did in fact recognize that long pass as my favorite play. I was standing in a corner trying to figure out which girl was most likely to tolerate my poor dancing when the fullback from our main rival team accosted me with his typical arrogance—and with two or three drinks already dancing in his head. This was late in 1940 and after I had been chosen by writers and coaches as the "All Mexico" quarterback. He had a different opinion from those who had labeled me the best. "You haven't really been such a good quarterback."

I realized he was at least half-drunk and so my answer was in good humor: "Why do you think I wasn't so good?"

"Because you didn't even have to use strategy. Whenever your team got stopped, you just faded back and threw that long pass to Salas and that got you out of the hole."

"And you don't think that it was good strategy?"

"Of course, not," he answered with a sarcastic tone.

I laughed and asked him if using the strongest play, when needed, was not good strategy. Seeing how angry this answer made him, I walked away and asked his sister to dance with me, which she did for at least a couple of dances. I think I proved to him that I had good strategy for dancing partners, at least.

Since we had several formations and different pass plays in each, I was able to keep almost all our opponents off balance and unable to break up our passing game.

My first high school championship game was in an old and almost venerated soccer stadium, "El Parque España." During my years of convalescence I had seen José Martínez Zorrilla play there. As a halfback at Cornell University, he had been the only Mexican (born in Mex-

ico) to ever win the "All-America" title in the U.S. I had watched him in envy and in sadness at a time when I believed that I would never again play football. Now, in the Spring of 1939, I was running out on the grass of that same stadium where I had admired Martínez Zorrilla. And I was the starting quarterback for my team.

It was one of those moments that a young man never forgets. I made it all the more memorable and exciting by calling for that long pass, number 90, on the first down of our first possession of the ball. Less than three minutes into that game and we already had a touchdown! Nobody seemed to expect a rookie quarterback to pass on the first play of his first game. Both sides of the stadium were silent for a few moments after that touchdown, as if they were in shock. And then our student body let out a roar that reminded me of the words "Shake down the thunder from the skies" in the old Notre Dame victory march.

Our opponents were from the prestigious National Preparatory School and it was a special joy for me to see that they were indeed in shock. After our surprise touchdown, they received our kickoff and went nowhere with it. In fact they went nowhere all afternoon. They did not cross mid-field into our side even once that afternoon. On our second possession I threw two short passes from our regular punt formation. That brought us up somewhere near their goal, about ten or fifteen yards away. There I changed to the Stanford double wingback formation, catching them off guard again, this time with a double reverse that they had never seen and certainly didn't expect. Our right halfback ran into the end zone without an opponent even near him. That was a marvelous afternoon. My mother was in the stands, the sun was shining in my

face, and our maroon and white uniforms looked beautiful to me. I felt as if I had reached the major leagues, which in a sense I had.

The only problem that I had during those days was that the school could not afford good football shoes. Those were made in the U. S. and were very expensive. This shoe problem directly affected the professional vocation of my younger brother, Guillermo. He was a tackle on that team, but he was already in college and his heart was in his studies. After that first wonderful victory, I found out that he had a pair of almost brand-new American football shoes. He had saved up for a long time to buy them, but he was only playing as a substitute. I had a very nice kit for the building of a model of the beautiful Hawker Fury airplane. It was a masterpiece of a kit, but that year I had more interest in football than in model airplanes. So I offered to trade the kit for his shoes and he accepted. By the following week, his entire room was covered with photographs of the great airplanes of the 1930s. He had cut them out from aviation journals he had been saving, and now even the ceiling of his bedroom was covered with airplane photographs. He was rather aloof from the rest of the family, living in the room over our garage, and seemed content to be alone most of the time. Actually, he was just very independent. He suddenly announced that he was changing his major from electrical to aeronautical engineering. I remember my father trying to dissuade him on the grounds that there was no designing nor building of airplanes in Mexico. Guillermo was steadfast in his decision and enrolled (with only one classmate) in the division of aeronautics of his college. He went on to become an outstanding student in that science and I went on to more

and better football.

Our "Politécnico" team won each of the remaining six games of the regular 1939 season. But pride does come before a fall. Just as we were feeling invincible, after winning the public school championship, we came to a playoff against a team from a private club. Most of the players on that team were from affluent families and that turned out to be important. What is seldom, if ever, a factor in the U. S. was very important in Mexico back then. There was a significant difference in the nutritional status of their players and ours. Our players were almost all from working-class families. A good number of them had very scanty breakfasts and could not afford to buy much more than an occasional sandwich or taco in our school cafeteria or in the little food stands that surrounded most schools in Mexico City.

It was not, however, the nutritional superiority of that team that worried me at the end of the 1939 season. I did not recognize it until later when I saw their size and checked their weights. That was the "Wachachara Club," and we all knew they were from affluent families. What worried me at the time of that game was that they were experienced players who had played together for three seasons. They were also faster, in spite of being bigger. They outweighed us by 15 to 20 pounds at almost every position.

I had seen them win the city championship the year before, and I must confess that I went into that game feeling that they were almost surely a better team. That was a disastrous frame of mind, one that a quarterback should never have and one that I never again allowed myself to harbor. There can be little doubt that it was precisely those

feelings that led directly to our defeat. For it was two of my mistakes that allowed them to make the two touchdowns that were the margin of their victory.

Near the end of the first half in a scoreless game, their running halfback started to run around our left end. Knowing that the halfback was a good runner, and forgetting that he was also a good passer, I rushed up to the line to help in stopping his run. As I neared the line, he saw me and faded back very rapidly to throw a perfect pass to their left end, who was all alone in the zone I had just vacated. They were already wearing us down with their fierce tackling and crisp blocking. They were executing well and we were executing with the mistakes that come from despair. I tried short passes to every one of my receivers, but most fell incomplete because I was tense and trying too hard, and also because they were giving me little time to set, aim and throw. Their big linemen were pounding me harder than I had ever been hit. The rules in those days did not protect the passer to the extent they do now, and so they could hit me long after I had thrown those short passes. Our blocking was very poor that day and our runners made only short gains all afternoon. It was almost the exact opposite of our first great victory. Our opponents were indeed bigger and faster than us, but it was their determination and their execution that won the game.

Near the end of the game, I threw what was supposed to be a "shovel pass" to my right halfback. Since we were getting nowhere with the regular pass plays, I tried this trick pass. The trouble was that someone came through our line and pushed my halfback out of the way just as he was about to come running parallel to our line to receive my pass. Instead, it was intercepted by their right guard and he just outran me to the goal.

I gave up only four interceptions in five seasons—still a record in Mexico—but that one was decisive. It led to our most painful defeat and left me looking incompetent, which is exactly what I was that afternoon. It was my lack of faith in our ability that was the most important factor in that defeat. The fact that we lost by only 14 to 0 is a tribute to the tenacity of our outweighed linemen.

For a school football team, the worst part of losing a championship is that you have to face your classmates and your whole school the following Monday. The family tries to cheer you up with all kinds of excuses, but classmates can be ruthless. Since non-players have little idea of what it is to face constant hard blows while trying to execute complex patterns of plays with precise timing, they seem to find it easy to ridicule defeated schoolmates. I knew this, and went to my classes for several days in a downcast mood. My pride had been as battered as my body. It was painful enough to make me vow that I would never again abandon my safety position on defense and that every opponent would have a hard time completing passes into my zone.

My mother let a few days go by without saying much and then she gave me a good-humored lecture about my great good fortune in having gone from a sick bed to the best stadiums of a large city. She also ordered me back for more mathematics tutoring with my uncle.

In the interim, Mexico was to have a presidential election in July of that year and my father was deeply involved in what was to be a dangerous, painful struggle. During the winter of 1939, I saw a Japanese gentleman handing some documents to my father in our living room.

No sooner had the Japanese man left then my mother burst out in anger. Her outburst alerted me to the dangers my father and the nation were in. But I was a young man in the flower of my youth and thinking my own selfish thoughts and not much about the struggles the world was facing exactly two years before Pearl Harbor. I was so determined to become the best quarterback in Mexico that I concentrated on that and not on my studies.

Sports writers agree that 1940 was the year in which American Football became popular in Mexico. When that year began, two soccer stadiums were converted for football by adding the different type goal posts and marking off the hundred-yard gridiron on the turf. The two other stadiums we used were small and uncomfortable. One, which seated only 5,000 spectators, was our school's concrete stadium, Estadio Camino Díaz, named in honor of some long forgotten professor. And then there was the old, half-finished Estadio Nacional (National Stadium) which seated some 20,000 fans. Both these stadiums had dirt playing fields because there had not been enough interest in maintaining the grass on them. Those neglected fields were so hard that they led to many an injury.

As I said earlier, in one single site we had a junior high school (including a trade school with large shops that looked like barns), a high school, and a college. It also had a large building for the one professional school on campus, the School of Architecture. It was considered one of the achievements of the Revolution of 1910, and the old revolutionaries like my father were very proud of that big school.

My second year of high school football was played in the spring of 1940. I especially felt that I had to make up for the previous year's loss to Wachachara. We had to play six games against the public schools, followed by a game against that club and finally a game against the National Preparatory School. Coach Mendiola was very conservative, and the only thing that convinced him to stress passing over running plays was the great success in the United States of those great passers Sammy Baugh of Texas, Frankie Albert of Stanford and Sid Luckman of Columbia University in New York.

In order to show my faith in the passing game, I started the season by calling for a long pass on the first play of the first game of the season. We had received the kickoff, which sailed over our heads, and had to start from our own twenty-yard line. I threw the ball about thirty yards to Juan José Salas and he carried it the rest of the way for an eighty-yard touchdown play. That set the tone for five more consecutive victories before our game against Wachachara. In every one of those five victories, I literally filled the air with passes.

When we came to the game against my nemesis of the year before, I was ready and anxious to play well. It was no longer just a desire to overcome serious illness that drove me. That afternoon I had a fierce determination to lead my team to victory. There was no platooning from offensive units to defensive units in those days. That meant that I would play quarterback on offense and deep safety on defense. And that would give me the opportunity to make up for the touchdown that they had scored on us when I had left my safety position empty the year before. I could not have dreamed that I would get as many opportunities as I actually did that memorable afternoon. Their team was as good or better than their 1939 outfit. They now had Julián Amezcua as a running back and he had just won both the 100 and the 200 meter dashes at the Pan American Games. He was, without hyperbole, "the fastest runner in the Americas." We faced a rather awesome challenge. They should have won. Fierce pride and determination on our team and a foolish strategy on their's decided the issue. That day, the few spectators in the old National Stadium saw football at it's best: two equally matched teams balancing their strengths. They had the fastest running back and we had the better passing game. The newspapers had goaded Amezcua saying that he could not stand up to the four quarters of pounding that our now experienced line would give him. They predicted that we would win because our passing was "far superior." And so, in foolish arrogance, Julián Amezcua decided to engage me in a passing duel.

He could have run circles around us, but he was a quarterback and felt an intense rivalry with me. On their first possession, he tried to do what I frequently did; he threw a long forward pass. Expecting him to do just that, I followed his deep receiver closely, stepped in front of him, and intercepted the pass. Since we were indeed evenly matched, the rest of the game was dominated by strong defenses. My first pass was dropped by Salas in the opponent's end zone, canceling a sure touchdown. Their defensive linemen were rushing me like fiends, and so I did not have time for long passes. I was completing passes, but they were short ones and we didn't score at all during the entire first half.

I was playing cautiously because I felt that they would eventually tire and allow Salas, or another of my receivers, to outrun them for our number 90 pass. Amezcua continued for too long with his passing game, and so I kept on intercepting. By the end of the first half, Julián Amezcua, quarterback for Wachachara, had thrown five passes and Jorge "Pocho" Prieto, quarterback for Politécnico, had intercepted all five. Amezcua was stubborn and proud. The Pan-American victories had gone to his head and he apparently was determined to prove that he was as good a passer as I was. He was a great runner, but that day he was obsessed with trying to show me up. He did momentarily come to his senses just before the half. He called for an end run from our thirty-yard line and simply outran all of us to the goal line.

That end run by Amezcua put them ahead 7 to 0. But it didn't change his desire to outpass me. I don't understand why his coach didn't convince him to forget the passing attack and continue to run around our ends. It was true that we had some very good ends and that we had placed them out wide with a halfback in close support. But end runs were still his best card.

Emotion is important in football, and we came out for the last half as fired up as any team ever returned from that short rest. Our blockers cleared a path for our kickoff receiver and he returned it all the way to midfield. That gave us a feeling of how strong we really were. On the first play I called for the number 90 pass and called it with so much vigor that every face in the huddle seemed to light up. But our opponents were prepared for a long pass, since I so frequently did that on first down, and they had Salas and Roberto Suárez, my other reliable receiver, very well covered. I had to scramble around a good while until I suddenly saw another of my receivers open. With a hard toss and with a whispered prayer, I threw it more than thirty yards and a rookie receiver carried it the final twenty for a touchdown.

Our passing had matched their running and our morale instantly improved. We were still, however, tied at 7 to 7.

We caught fire so well after that sudden touchdown that we were able to contain Amezcua for the rest of the afternoon. Being stopped cold forced him to fall back on his previously unsuccessful passing game. In the third quarter, he threw three more. I intercepted two and the other one fell incomplete. We came to the last five minutes of game time deadlocked 7 to 7.

By now Wachachara was visibly tired and its linemen were no longer rushing me as strongly as in the first half. Noticing this, and with the ball in our possession on our forty-yard line, I called for two quick short passes followed by the long crossover number 90. All three passes were complete and with the third one, to Suárez, we scored, making it 14 to 7 in our favor. This took a bit more than three minutes, and so they would have only one more chance to score. They tried two running plays, which our determined linemen stopped cold, and then Amezcua threw his ninth long pass. I intercepted him—for the eighth time—and ran it back to their ten yard line. As Julián Amezcua tackled me there, I turned, saw my teammate Suárez off to one side and behind me, and threw him a lateral pass which he carried to a touchdown. The referee ruled that one of my knees had touched the ground before the lateral and ruled the ball dead on their ten-yard line. And so we won by only 14 to 7.

My schoolmates came down from the stands, put me on their shoulders, and carried me twice around the field

and then deposited me at the main entrance to that old stadium where my mother was waiting with the expected tears in her eyes. But those were tears of joy. We both knew that it was more then a victory in a well played game. We had truly overcome. This was as good a reply to her challenge to me back in that Plaza in San Luis as either of us could have expected.

We all need encouragement now and then. Children, adolescents and the elderly specially need to be told that they are "good." That afternoon it seemed that everyone I saw was telling me how "good" I was.

Our whole team, including that rookie who had caught his first touchdown pass, felt that we were indeed very good athletes. For me, football had become a sport where I could test myself against young men usually bigger and faster than I was. The knowledge that I had overcome a serious illness made each game all that more exciting and every victory more exhilarating.

Our final game that spring season of 1940 was against another traditional rival, the Escuela Nacional Preparatoria. That was a coeducational high school with more than two thousand students. At least half of those were young males, but they had not found in all that mass of students a single really good passer. They had a good team otherwise. They had a line made up of very large, heavy players and had some very fast running backs. We had been able to hold "the fastest man in the Americas" to only one touchdown the week before and, therefore, I went into my final high school game with the conviction that we would win.

As we ran out on the field that afternoon, the roar of our student body was an emotional reminder of the great

victory of the week before.

It was the springtime of the year and the springtime of my life. The best description of how I felt that afternoon can be found in "The Hound of Heaven" by Francis Thompson, where he wrote "In the rash lustihead of my young powers, I shook the pillaring hours."

I did shake some "pillaring hours" that afternoon, throwing several touchdown passes and getting at least one record for a punt return that has never been matched.

But not everything I did that afternoon reflected athletic ability or quarterbacking wisdom. Not only did I make mistakes, I made a really unusual one. Our opponents had purple uniforms. Ours were maroon and white. The difference in colors was such that it should have been almost impossible to make the mistake I made.

I was so sure of our superiority that I called a dangerous play and executed it in a manner as dumb as dumb can be. We had taken the kickoff and literally smashed our way down to their three-yard line. With first down and goal to go, I called the most complicated play in our playbook: a reverse from the Stanford double wingback formation. That play called for a great deal of lateral running, parallel to the line of scrimmage. It is best used near midfield, when the opponents usually charge cautiously for fear of a pass. It also takes precise timing.

Just as I was about to give the reverse to one of my running wingbacks, the opposing left end came rushing in and I handed the ball off to him! He was so surprised at my gift of that football that he hesitated before starting to run towards our goal. This gave one of our backs the chance to catch up and tackle him before he had gone too far. The arrogant confidence I had felt until that moment was transformed into the realization every football player should have of the possibility of losing any game. Regardless of what sportswriters may say, it only takes a couple of mistakes for a favored team to lose. The linesman that received my "gift" reverse did not score, nor did any other of our opponents score on us that day. We had them baffled by the changes in formations, changes which I made constantly.

We were outweighed, but they were outplayed. I was able to complete three passes for touchdowns. That game produced the longest punt return in the history of football in Mexico, where it had been played since 1927. A defensive safety normally does not try to return a punt that is about to land inside his own five-yard line. It is too dangerous because the safety has his eyes on the ball coming down from the sky while the opposing linemen, with many yards of momentum, generally arrive almost simultaneously with the ball. It is easy to fumble under those circumstances and a fumble so near your own goal is usually disastrous. I knew all this, but my first two touchdown passes had made me regain my confidence. I wanted to win so convincingly that I risked the fumble and fielded that punt and ran over or around all eleven of those purple jerseys. A 99-yard punt return for a touchdown! My brother Guillermo was on the field at the time and he ran interference for me. As I broke into the clear, with only the enemy punter between me and the goal line, I saw his big number 23 leading me. He was waving his right arm, signaling for me to follow him. I felt a surge of happiness at seeing him clearing the way, as he did, by blocking the last obstacle and leading me to the goal line.

Our coach gave me a reprimand at the half for taking such a risk, but he did mumble something about good open-field running. With that record punt return, we were ahead three touchdowns to zero. That afternoon was my brother Guillermo's best game ever. Not only did he furnish the interference that took me to the goal on that long punt return, he also stopped our opponent's" only real challenge of the game. Early in the third quarter, when the enemy could still have made a contest of it, Guillermo stopped them cold. In their desperation to get back into contention, Preparatoria had been able to march all the way down to our five-yard line. There, they tried an off-tackle run to the side where my brother was playing defensive tackle. Guillermo broke through their blockers and met their best running back head on. He hit him so hard that he not only stopped him cold, he made him fumble the ball. Another of our linesmen recovered and we all knew that they had given their best effort and failed. After that, I threw short and long passes from all of our five formations and completed most of them. We were a happy family that glorious afternoon. Every young athlete should have at least one day of triumph, a day when every effort proves ability and determination can win.

We won 28 to 0, and I went home believing that I would be accepted as the varsity college quarterback in the fall. We were the 1940 high school city champions, and I must have been strutting like a little rooster because my mother put that game in a more balanced perspective with an exchange that went something like this:

"How did you like the game, Mom?"

"Well . . . it was a good game, but I don't think I will go see any more of your games after today's."

"Why not, we won by a lot and played real well, didn't we?"

"Not as well as you are thinking right now. Remember what you did the first time you came near their goal, when you gave the ball to a player on the other team?"

"Oh, that play. But we caught up with him and they didn't score."

"He didn't score, but you should have heard what your own classmates in the stands were shouting about me! I felt like hitting them with my umbrella, but I didn't want them to know that I was your mother." And they were right in being angry at that foolish play. You lost a chance for a touchdown."

"But you don't understand, mom, that when we get to a certain number in my counting, I am supposed to hand the ball to the player running by me. He just happened to be the wrong one."

"Excuses, excuses. Your jerseys are all white and theirs were a bright purple. You could not have been more different. Did you have your eyes closed?"

She said all this with a smile and with the look of a mother that is very happy. We were sharing the joys of another great victory.

I was apparently as healthy as I had ever been since that episode of cardiac illness in 1935, but there was a time-bomb ticking away in my abdomen. The appendicitis that was to reach a climax in a couple of days was already starting on the Saturday of the game. I had felt a sudden weakness in my right leg when an opponent, trying to block me, gave me a bump on my right hip. It made me feel so weak that I fell to the grass. I knew there was something wrong with my right side, but the excitement of the game made me forget it, and I played the complete four quarters on offense and on the defense, as usual.

The pain in my abdomen did not start until Monday morning on my way to school. I no sooner reached school than I realized I had to return home in San Angel, a suburb more than twenty miles from my school. The pain and the nausea were very bad and became progressively worse on the long trip back home. At least twice I had to get off the buses to go to the curbside and vomit. That trip seemed endless, but I finally made it back home. I had heard, of course, that people with appendicitis sometimes have their appendix rupture and then develop something called "peritonitis," which usually brought their death. This was before the era of antibiotics and a lot of people did die from appendicitis.

Naturally, I could not be sure that I had appendicitis, but I had heard it described when I was living with my uncle in San Luis. One of those two pretty girls in that family of thirteen children had died from a ruptured appendix. I was now wondering if my appendix would rupture too. Fortunately, I was young, strong, and in otherwise general good health. That damaged heart valve could complicate matters, but I was sure I would make it if they got me to a hospital quickly.

My mother called an elderly general practitioner from the neighborhood. That same summer of 1935, when my rheumataic fever began, my mother had done a good amount of medical reading that summer and actually was very knowledgeable about medicine. It was rather funny hearing her exchange opinions with that doctor. When he said, "This young man has acute appendicitis and we have to get him to a surgeon at once," my mother said something to the effect, "Don't you need a blood count on him to confirm that diagnosis?" The good doctor was probably used to dealing with amateur "doctors." He took the medical advice calmly and I remember that he said, "Señora Prieto, this young man has appendicitis, with or without a blood count." My mother was wise enough to stop challenging him. I was getting progressively worse, with almost constant retching. The only problem was the fact that we didn't know any general surgeon. A teammate of mine was the nephew of a famous neurosurgeon, so we called him. This is how it turned out that my appendix was removed by a brain surgeon.

I was taken to a small orthopedic hospital and rushed to the operating room. I remember they took a sample of my blood, but it was when I was already in surgery. The appendix had indeed ruptured in route. Because they could not find a regular anesthesiologist, an orthopedic surgeon gave me a spinal anesthesia.

It was fascinating to be awake while they operated on me. The big overhead lamp, the sounds of the instruments as they were returned to their tray, and the muffled voices of the surgeon and his assistants speaking through their masks all seemed very dramatic to that young quarterback. Little did he know that the glamour of operating rooms was to appeal to him for the rest of his life. That operation was a true adventure for a young man. Early into the procedure I asked about the foul smell that had suddenly filled the room. Dr. Mariano Vásquez, the famous brain surgeon, heard my complaint and said, "That smell is you, so be quiet." It was true, of course, because I had a belly-full of pus with the peritonitis that goes with a ruptured appendix. I realized it could have ruptured during the game, two days

before. But 1940 was my lucky year and I had no complications, damaged heart valve and all. This, as I have mentioned, was before penicillin, but I recovered and was up and about in less than a week.

In the spring of 1940 I had not seriously considered a career in medicine, but I am sure that the experience of that successful operation had some influence in my eventual choice of a career. Dr. Noyola of San Luis had already given me an example of enthusiasm for the great profession of physician and surgeon, but that spring I was thinking mostly about football and hoping that some beautiful girl could fall in love with me.

So engrossed was I with those two obsessions that my studies suffered greatly. My interest in science, especially in biology and chemistry, was there, but a degree in any science was far off while pretty girls seemed to be everywhere.

I had crooked front teeth and was a very poor dancer. Both these conditions worried me to the point of believing that they were the reason for my lack of romantic success. There were no orthodontists in those days, nor could we have afforded the services of one. There were also no masks on football helmets at the time. I was lucky that I didn't get those front teeth knocked out in my five seasons of play.

The appendicitis episode kept me out of school for two months. It also probably saved me from a confrontation with my father. I had studied less than I should have before the operation and my grades in Chemistry and in Analytic Geometry were just enough to pass at mid-year. And even those grades were gifts from two professors who were avid fans of our football team. I was leaving all my

energies and a good deal of my time on the football field.

What actually saved me from my father's wrath was that he was engaged in organizing a national political party to present serious opposition to the omnipotent state party. He was, in fact, doing more than just organizing a new party; he and the surviving revolutionaries were conspiring to start a revolution all over again.

The ideals of 1910 had been given little more than lip service in the speeches of government officials, and those old revolutionaries thought that a national election in 1940 was an ideal time to establish a democratic government. I did not understand until much later why the historian Daniel Cosío Villegas wrote in his *La sucesión presidencial en México* (Presidential Succession in Mexico): "There was little doubt that in 1940 Jorge Prieto Laurens was, as he had been in 1923, the most dangerous man in Mexico."

Knowing that my father was busy with all those political activities, I decided to risk my academic standing by playing two seasons of football in the same year. College football was in the fall and so in August of 1940 I came out to the practice field and asked Coach Salvador Mendiola if he would let me try out for varsity college quarterback. He had been my coach those two seasons of high school football and he wanted me on the college team as soon as possible. I knew that and also knew they did not have a team physician, except at games. So, once again, nobody would hear my heart murmur.

Coach Mendiola had been training those Politécnico teams for only two years and had yet to win the national championship. Perhaps that was why he neglected to inquire if I had graduated from high school. I had not, but nobody asked. My dream of becoming the varsity quarterback for a major college was about to become reality. Thank God for disorganization, or poorly enforced regulations!

With World War II already sweeping Europe and a revolution brewing in Mexico, football should have been a very minor consideration for all of us. For me it was the goal I had dreamed about since I was a boy on the streets of Los Angeles.

I spent some rather strange days alone with my father in hiding during the summer of 1940. The elections for president and for congress had been held on July 7th of that year. Twenty-nine people were killed at the voting polls in Mexico City alone. The deaths in the states and territories were never reported in the press. The federal government obviously felt that it could kill with impunity. Or it must have thought that it could put down the rebellion the old revolutionaries were planning if the voting was again fraudulent, as it had been since 1924.

I finally understood the tumultuous welcome that my father had received at the railroad terminal in 1933. The people of Mexico were looking for leadership. That leadership emerged in the campaign for the presidency in 1939-1940. I remember a talk my father and I had during those days in hiding.

"Why are you willing to risk so much, dad?"

"Because if we don't fight for the ideals of the Revolution, people will lose all interest and the government will continue to feel that it is not accountable".

"What happens if the government is not accountable?"

"When they know that the voters can't make them

accountable, they continue to steal everything, as they have been doing for years. That is why there is so much corruption in Mexico."

"And how are you going to change that?"

"By forcing them to respect the people's vote"

He didn't explain how this was going to come about, but we both knew that he was thinking of doing it the way the nation had done in 1910 to get rid of the dictator, Porfirio Díaz. That meant starting another revolution, and each time this was mentioned, I felt great dismay. The thought of violence and the dangers to my father, to his followers, and to the whole nation dismayed me. I also felt a great sadness knowing that another revolution would probably be defeated by U.S. aid to our corrupt government.

That talk with my father was one of the best lessons about democracy I ever received. I had shared my mother's fears when he was crossing the border with contraband dynamite in 1929. Now I was seeing him risk his life all over again for the same love of freedom that only democracy can bring to a nation.

Somehow the conspirators in 1940 thought they could overcome White House opposition, just as President Venustiano Carranza had been able to do in 1917. Watching my dad, I had a first-hand opportunity to see national and international politics at work.

Enjoying life in general as much as I did that year, I could not believe that Mexico might erupt in violence again. The precautions my father was taking in hiding seemed excessive. We were hiding in the home of an American newspaperman in an isolated suburb. We were on a little side street, Calle de Penunuri, that was still

paved with sixteenth-century cobblestones. That suburb was at the extreme southern edge of the city and still very isolated. The conqueror Hernán Cortez had lived in a large home nearby. That building where he had once lived still existed. Those icons of our history gave our hideaway an erie sense of mystery. Having to hide in a neighborhood with churches, homes, and buildings that had been there for more than four centuries made me brood over the fate of a nation that has had so much to overcome. It made me proud, but it also made me worry about Mexico's destiny.

The lonely, narrow, and quiet streets were a reminder of Mexico's tortured history. They seemed like another world to me. The streets were mostly still paved with the cobblestones put there by the conquistadores. The homes still had the names of Diego de Ordaz, Pedro de Alvarado, Hernan Cortez and all those adventurers who had come long ago with the Cross of Christ in one hand and the sword in the other.

We spent most of our time in Mr. Gibler's basement. At least my father did. I went out every morning to get him the newspapers. I also made a semblance of keeping up with my studies. My school was at the other end of town and the only classes I attended with regularity were Mathematics, Chemistry, and Logic. This last subject was taught by the great teacher Dr. Demetrio Sokolov, and his were the only classes I never missed. That, I realized was not logical behavior for someone striving to become a college student, but it was a "crazy" year and I was charged with watching over my dad's safety and reporting back to the rest of the family.

Mr. Gibler was somewhat like Ambrose Bierce insofar as he made a career of following Mexican revolutionaries up close. Sometimes he seemed to understand Mexico better than I did, which was understandable, given his age. Frank Gibler was an experienced journalist and in listening to him discuss international politics with my father, I was listening to two intelligent and courageous men discuss the tortuous history of the two nations. All this was approximately a year before Pearl Harbor.

My father would review all the newspapers every day, underlining and cutting out the items important to him. He would take phone calls, make notes, and, incidentally, listen to Winston Churchill over what was then called the "short wave radio." That is how I came to have the unusual experience of hearing that great British statesman in some of his most important wartime speeches. Churchill understood the drama of politics and he used the radio effectively. He would say, "I am going to be silent for a few moments so that you can hear the terrorist bombing that the Nazi air force is inflicting on the people of London." While he remained silent, we could hear the explosions of those bombs. He would then resume, always saying something to the effect that the British would never surrender. That was one of the important lessons of my youthful years. Seeing my father cope so serenely with his dangerous isolation and hearing Winston Churchill leading his nation in wartime were parts of the same cloth. Both of them were fighting for democracy.

One morning in early August of that year, I went out for the newspapers and saw a headline about a General Zarzosa having been shot to death in the northern city of Monterrey. There were also pictures of the murdered general in his pajamas stained with the blood from the assassin's bullets. That military officer was the number two man

in the opposition party. As secretary general of the opposition party, my father became the number two man. Only the presidential candidate outranked him. That morning, I understood why we were in hiding. My father loved to walk, but during those weeks in Coyoacán he accepted what was almost imprisonment. He had seen many of his friends and colleagues suffer violent deaths during the Revolution. However, he took Zarzosa's death with a peculiar mixture of serenity and anger. I had never seen such anger in him. I didn't learn much math that year, but I certainly learned something about the price of democracy.

We waited in Mr. Gibler's basement until the White House decided that having the security of Mexico's oil reserves was more important than democracy in Mexico. President Roosevelt did this by simply announcing that he was sending Vice President Henry Wallace to the inauguration of President-Elect Manuel Avila Camacho—he had received so few votes that the people joked that even his mother did not vote for him. I was with my father when the news of that diplomatic recognition was transmitted over the radio. My father simply said with great sadness, "It is all over." That was one of the saddest days of my life. It didn't diminish my determination to become a college quarterback, it just placed it in a more proper perspective. It made me realize how war changes ideals such as democracy into excuses for security. I was being a witness to that ancient adage that "the first casualty of any war is always the truth." I also came to realize how much power the presidents in the White House have over other countries and how they can use or abuse it. I had heard my father say this many times during our ten years in exile, but now, in 1940, I was a personal witness to the use of

that awesome power over smaller and weaker nations.

On my return to classes in September, I decided to take all the subjects required of a high school third-year student as well as the two, Analytic Geometry and Inorganic Chemistry, for which I had been given a passing grade from professors who were better sports fans than they were teachers. My mother knew that I, once more, had been going to get mathematics tutoring on weekends. Both my tutor, the old colonel, and my mother knew of my obsession to play college football. They asked for my reasons for repeating those two subjects and were somewhat surprised when I told them that I was ashamed of the gift of passing grades given by the chemistry and math professors. I really wanted to learn those two important subjects.

In order to catch up with the classwork missed during those three or four weeks spent in hiding, I was forced to miss the first two games of the college season. Thus, when Coach Mendiola accepted me for my tryout, our team already had one loss and one tie. I felt guilty and worried. The upcoming game was to be against our main rival, the National University of Mexico. They had been champions for seven consecutive years and had a very good team. They had good passers and good runners, all of them veterans of at least three years of college ball. Their best runner was a veteran of more than six years as a player and an equal number of years as a part-time medical student. I was going to face them as a rookie with just two years of high school experience.

As chance and bad luck would have it, I faced a tough exam in chemistry on the Friday before my first college game. What made it bad luck was that the examination was to be supervised by the same teacher who had

given me an unearned passing grade the previous spring. This time I had studied and gone to labs. I had studied so much that I did not show up for practice until after those first two games. I felt that I had to prove that I was not just a sports "jock."

I was ready for that test. What I was not ready for was the humiliation to which that teacher subjected me. As we started to write down our answers to the ten chemical equations on the blackboard, the teacher stood next to my desk and started to give me the answers. He did this in a voice that the whole class could hear!

I was shocked, to say the least. I turned and saw the angry, incredulous faces of my classmates. As it was, a few already disliked me because of my football fame. I solved that ridiculous situation by putting my pen back into my shirt pocket and walking out of the room. I left with anger because I was well prepared for that exam, and walking out on an examination is not something schools readily accept. I realized that this teacher wanted to help me, but he did it in such a gross, dishonest way that it humiliated both of us. What I did was as foolish as the wrong the teacher had done. It was also unnecessary.

I believed that I was doing the only right thing I could do and left that classroom to review the formations and plays for what I knew was be one of the decisive games of my life. If we lost my first game as varsity quarterback, my fame would fade almost instantly. Or I could establish myself as one of the best if we won. I spent a good part of that Friday afternoon walking back and forth in a little alley near my home. My youngest sister Teresita walked with me, trying to teach her oldest brother the prayers in Spanish that I needed to know in order to go to confession.

Obviously, I felt I needed Divine help in order to win against the perennial champions. I was taking my worries too seriously, but then most rookie quarterbacks do the same. I was also taking those worries to the only fountain of serenity I knew: my faith.

I was so worried, that after three or four failures to learn a prayer by heart, my little sister asked: "How come you remember your chemistry and your mathematics equations so well and you can't seem to learn a simple prayer?" I finally learned it, went into the Convento del Carmen church, confessed my sins, and came out light-hearted and confident.

There had been a vicious, almost slanderous controversy in the local newspapers during the entire week. The President of the National University had taken on the almost daily task of trying to demean our school. He called it a "second-class university," fit only for training "proletarians" in trades and not for students in the professions. As a unit, our school was new and we did indeed have a track that was just for those wishing to learn a trade. We had, however, as part of our school, the thirty-year old School of Electrical and Mechanical Engineering. That school had been producing competent professionals for all those years, as had our School of Business Administration. The President of the National University knew about those schools, but he chose to ignore them so as to make us appear inferior. He was a surgeon and known to have protested, vociferously, the inauguration of a School of Medicine at our Institute. This new professional school at the Politécnico was designed to train physicians for practice exclusively in the rural areas of Mexico. There had always been a grievous shortage of doctors in all rural areas of the nation, and this was a reasonable attempt to remedy that lack. But the arrogant surgeon at the head of the National University objected strenuously to creating another School of Medicine, and in the process he tried to make us look inferior in the public eye.

I was aware of those newspaper attacks because they made my father very angry. He considered our Instituto Politécnico to be one of the great achievements of his beloved Revolution, and he naturally resented the elitist slander against the school. I did not think it would have anything at all to do with our forthcoming big game that Saturday. It turned out otherwise.

As we ran out on the field of our little stadium to play against the National University, I saw the Director of all the Politécnico schools standing next to our bench on the sidelines. He was Colonel and Engineer Don Wilfrido Massieu, and all of us called him Don Wilfrido as a sign of our respect and esteem. It was well-merited esteem, I must say, since that elderly gentleman had a truly magnificent reputation. In civil war and in peace, as a soldier and as a professional, he had won the respect of all. He was the embodiment of integrity and the whole school loved him. During the Revolution he had defeated my father's fellow revolutionaries at almost every battle and had earned the rank of colonel on the battlefield. As the director of a large conglomerate of public schools, he was vigorous and competent.

And now he was standing on our sideline. I suddenly feared that he had come to tell me that I could not play because I had walked out on a teacher giving an exam. But he was not there to punish me. He had come to motivate me! I started to try explaining my behavior at that chem-

istry exam and he interrupted me gently, saying, "Don't worry about that. I heard what happened, and you did the right thing. I'll see that you get another exam with someone else when you are ready. He then said something about football not really having anything to do with the quality of a school, but that nevertheless it was seen by the general public as a sign of "strength" and therefore important. He asked me if I had been reading about the controversy between him and Dr. Gustavo Baz of the National University. I answered that I certainly had been reading about it. And he said that he knew I would play courageously since both he and my father expected nothing less. He then told me that the reason he had come to our bench was to ask me to lead our team to victory! The victory that was obviously important to him and to our entire school.

Up until that moment I had been as worried as any rookie quarterback about to call his first game. Don Wilfrido's words changed my personal worries into a serene determination to win.

It turned out to be one of the hardest fought games in the history of American football in Mexico. They were defending their many years of supremacy, and we were fighting to make our school respected. At least that is what I felt as we lined up for the kickoff.

For me, the game began on a very ominous note. On our first possession on our own thirty-yard line, I called for a fake reverse with me spinning into the line and carrying the ball. I wanted to prove that the anonymous phone calls of the whole week threatening me with bodily harm had not intimidated me. I proved my point, but they got just what they wanted. They hurt me almost enough to incapacitate me on that very first play. As I spun around and crossed their line, tacklers hit me from both sides and somebody on their team yelled as I was falling, "Hit him on the head, hit him on the head." That is exactly what one of their players did. He gave me such a hard blow with his knee to my leather helmet that my head bounced on that hard turf. As I got up, everything looked blurred; the people in the stands and even the players on our nearby bench were just a vague mass. I couldn't focus on objects even ten yards away. I also could not tell exactly where my ankles or my knees were. Obviously, I had a brain concussion and should have left the field at once. Fortunately, one of my halfbacks noticed my difficulty in getting up and called for a time-out. He then started making believe he was drawing a diagram on the dirt field, called me and the rest of the team to him, making out that he was suggesting a special play so as to distract attention from my condition and to give me time to recover. He was successful in giving me time to at least be able to walk steadily, even though the concussion lasted for most of the game. I felt very groggy, but I also felt I could not afford to leave the field after my first play.

My mother was in the stands, and I felt that I simply could not let her, or the opponents, see that I had been hurt. My teammates would have been discouraged, too. They were counting on my passing to win the game for them, and we had no other passer. So I did the only thing I could think of at the time. For the next two quarters of play I called only the strongest and simplest running plays, plays in which I did not have much more to do than hand off the ball to one of my running backs, or help block an opponent.

At the half our coach asked why I had not attempted

a single pass, and I told him that I was lulling them into a false sense of security with our strong running attack. I said that I wanted to catch them flatfooted with a long pass after they became overconfident and were bunched up near the line of scrimmage. I wasn't about to tell him that I had suffered a concussion and was just beginning to see straight. I was determined to win that game. My eyesight did not really clear up until about the middle of the third quarter. Both teams were tiring of the battering we were giving each other, and the opposition had indeed become overconfident in thinking I wasn't about to pass. It is possible that some of their linemen had noticed that I was unsteady on my feet after that first play and had relayed that information to their backfield. In any case, they did bunch up close to defend against our running plays. It worked out in such a way that my team, forever after, thought that I was a genius in strategy.

Near the end of the third quarter, our right tackle, a tough and sarcastic Yaqui Indian, asked me, "Whatever happened to your famous throwing arm?" I answered, as I had to the coach, that I was "setting the enemy backfield up to believe I would not pass."

By this time my sight had cleared so that I could see the people in the stands clearly and therefore knew I could throw a long pass accurately. On our next first down I called the old number 90 pass and found their entire backfield foolishly massed up on the line of scrimmage expecting another run. As I faded back, I saw my right end crossing deep towards the opponent's goal. He was all alone and I felt a sense of elation as I set my feet firmly and threw my first pass. My receiver did not even break stride as he reached up to catch that long spiral and ran the few

remaining yards for a touchdown. The demoralization of our opponents was visible and audible. They were swearing, mostly at each other. The unintended play had worked and the shock was just too much for the champions.

On our very next possession, knowing that they were still in a state of shock, I called the same pass, this time on second down after an eight-yard advance and, thus, when they had every reason to expect another run. In their anger and confusion, two of their backs followed our right end (the one that had just scored on them) and left my other end to cross to the other side all alone. So I threw my second touchdown pass of the afternoon.

After that, since I had developed a tremendous headache from the concussion, I went back to our simplest plays while our defense, undoubtedly full of adrenaline, had no difficulty in stopping their final efforts.

As I was coming off the field, Don Wilfrido, the old Colonel, came by me and gently patted my shoulder pads saying, "Great game, Jorge, great game."

Indeed, it had been a great game, greater even then my dreams. Making our dean, Don Wilfrido, happy and proud was just an extra bonus to a marvelous victory. I still marvel that I was able to pull it off in spite of the concussion. I had a rather severe headache for almost a week after that game, but I was a happy young man. I was the school hero and even gained new friends when I passed the chemistry exam a week later. Word got around about how I had refused the passing security from that professor. I had achieved my football dreams on my first try, and I had shown that I was a good student in a difficult subject.

Since our team had lost the first game of the season and the National University had won all their games before losing to us, we were, theoretically, equal or tied and had to play each other once more in order to decide the championship. And so, just two weeks after that great and exhausting game, we had to meet our main rivals once again. In the interim, I didn't have to worry about learning new prayers. I felt that we had to learn new plays.

Walking near the old National University School of Medicine shortly after our victory, I met Fernando Díaz. He was one of the University halfbacks who had failed to cover my receivers on both of those touchdown passes. He gave me what he thought was a dire warning, saying that I had best think twice before trying that crossover pass again in our upcoming game. "You fade back for that long pass again," he said, "and we will smash you to the ground before you have time to get rid of the ball." My answer was that he surely would not think me foolish enough to try the same play again.

Actually, he did me a great favor. The following day I went to our coach's home and convinced him that we could take advantage of their anxiety of trying to hit me as soon as I faded back for a long pass. I talked Coach Mendiola into approving that we try the very old, and hardly ever seen, "Statue-of-Liberty" play on our first passing opportunity. That play consists of the passer fading back as if to pass, raising the ball up as a passer must do, and having his left halfback come around from behind and snatch it from the passer's upraised arm. This only works if well-timed and if the defensive ends are rushing in hard. I had seen the California Institute of Technology use it successfully against U.C.L.A. way back in 1931. I was just a kid at that time, but I had a good memory and the threat by Fernando Díaz made it the logical play to try. If it worked, it could also help our passing attack since our opponents would not know when we would try it again and, therefore, would charge me with some hesitancy.

We knew that the National University team would come roaring out on the field, trying to erase the humiliation of their 14 to 0 defeat of the first game. I was sure that the first time they saw me fade back to throw a long pass, their defensive ends would converge on me, trying to tackle me before I could throw the ball. If they did that, their flanks would be unguarded since their linebackers would follow our receivers as they ran downfield. Those are ideal conditions for a successful "Statue-of-Liberty" play. There was a risk, of course. If one of their ends were to hit me before my halfback was near enough to take the ball off from my upraised arm, I would either be down for a loss or I would fumble. Therefore, we had to have our timing down to near perfection. We also had to have the rest of our team, as well as the opponents, believing that I was indeed about to pass. So it was that our left halfback, Roberto Suárez, our center and myself were the only ones, besides our coach, to know of the play. The four of us stayed over after practice every day of the two weeks before that game. We agreed that we would try the "Statue-of-Liberty" play on our first possession and that I would let only Roberto Suárez know it was not the number 90 pass which is what I would call in the huddle.

The National University team did come out like roaring lions for that second and decisive encounter with us. They won the coin toss, elected to receive, and marched right down the field with fierce determination. Without throwing a single pass, they just tore our defense apart with running plays. They were using the old Notre Dame shift with near perfection, until they reached our two-yard line. There, they took our defensive line and our linebackers by surprise. Instead of shifting into the box, as they always did, the center passed to their quarterback, standing right behind him in his normal position before the shift, and he ran it in for a touchdown while we were still waiting for them to shift. It was the "quarterback sneak," done when least expected.

After that, they obviously thought that all they had to do to win was to keep me from throwing long passes. They would kick off to us and rush me hard as soon as I faded back to pass. They followed that script to the letter, just as I had expected. On our first down, from our own twenty-yard line, I called number 90 but signaled to Roberto Suárez for the "Statue-of-Liberty." The opposing linemen did what I had predicted. Their defensive left end, Eliot Camarena, came rushing in like a tornado. He tackled me low and hard just as Roberto Suárez took the football from my upraised hand and ran past the undefended flank. As Camarena and I fell to the ground, he mocked me saying I was a fool to try a pass so near my own goal. He had, in fact, tackled me on our seven- or eight-yard line. I lay there on the ground and pointed to Suárez, who was just reaching midfield. They were so angered and confused by that strange play that I was immediately able to complete two short passes and a reverse running play followed by a fake pass with a lateral that scored a touchdown. This answered their score and tied us at 7 points each after we converted the extra point.

We were blocking, tackling, and running just as ferociously as they had been. They did not complete a single pass in the entire game, mostly because of our rushing of their passer. We were able to do what they had threatened to do. We just didn't give them time to pass at all. They in turn gave me very little time to pass as they had promised, but I found that I could complete quickly thrown short passes. They were indeed wary of another "Statue-of-Liberty" play.

For the second half, they changed to the new T-formation that we had never seen (except for that quarterback sneak). This new formation confused us enough so that with five minutes to go before the end of the game, they were able to score with another running play for a touchdown. But they missed the extra point and led by six, 13 to 7.

They weren't about to give up their many years of supremacy and we had very little time to score the 7 points needed to win the game and the national championship. They punted over our goal line and so we had four minutes left of play with the ball in our possession on our twenty-yard line. We had eighty yards to march through a determined team of veterans, and we only had four minutes to do it. With only one huddle, I called for three consecutive short passes followed by our longest pass. The three short ones were complete, but the long pass was dropped by our left end when he was out in the clear and could have scored. As we lined up in the huddle with the ball on the 50-yard line, the referee said to me, "You have only 8 seconds left, time for one more play." I looked across our huddle at Juan José Salas and he moved his head up and down, indicating that he was ready. He would have to run those fifty yards, evade the defense, and catch my pass if I could get it to him. Everybody in that stadium must have known that I was going to throw the long pass to Salas. The opponents knew it so well that they had placed their three best backfield men way back on their own goal line. This time there could be no surprise worked on them. And there was no doubt that their defensive line was going to rush me with the fervor of a last chance to stop me from throwing long. Afterwards, I learned that most betting people in the stands had paid off their bets already, as if the National University had already won.

My mother told me later that before that last play she was leaving the stands in tears, thinking that we had lost. As she and most other spectators started to file out, my friend Rafael Lizardi, who had sat next to her all during the game, said, "Sit down, Señora, Jorge is going to do exactly what that Notre Dame player did five years ago against Ohio State. He is going to throw a touchdown pass on the last play of the game." So she sat down and saw her son do what should have been impossible: complete a pass of more than fifty yards against a defense that knew exactly what he was going to do and which receiver they had to cover. We were so far from their goal line that I had to give my receiver time enough to run at least fifty yards and then cross to the other sideline and get behind their defensive backs. True, of course, that Salas and I had been using that play since our days in junior high school, but never against players so experienced and never against linemen as big and as determined as the ones who rushed me in the twilight of that afternoon. I scrambled first to the sideline to my right, spun around giving ground, and ran until I was near the other sideline where our student body and my mother were watching. Less than two seconds before those giants hit me, I sent a long spiral across that darkening sky. It landed in the outstretched hands of Juan José Salas, who leaped as high as he ever did just as all

three defensive enemy backs hit him. He was hit probably as hard as the defensive linemen had just hit me, but he did not drop the ball and landed behind their goal line. We were tied 13 to 13 with the national champions!

Pandemonium broke loose. People were fighting because bets had already been paid before the pass and nobody knew who won those bets in case of a tie. In the darkness of the dying afternoon, we could not find the football. Teams in those days were not affluent and usually had only one or two footballs. The madness was such that I had to convince the referee, Mr. Uruchurtu, that we had not won but were only tied and still entitled to try the point after touchdown. Uruchurtu had been my predecessor as quarterback for Politécnico and he was as excited as the spectators who thought that the pass had won the game.

We finally found the football—two students were fighting for it—and I thought I could take advantage of the other team's confusion. I tried the option play around the end for that point after touchdown. Our opponents turned out to be more angry than confused and they stopped the option cold on the scrimmage line. Their left end tackled our carrier, but in so doing had rushed off-side and gave us a second chance for the victory, and now from their one-yard line. Because the distance to traverse was so small, and because my right tackle assured me with vehemence, that he could open a hole in the opponent's line, I tried a run by our strongest fullback, following our right tackle.

The point after touchdown is best made by an experienced place-kicker, but our kicker was not on the field and I thought that our best blocking linesman, Yaqui Heredia, could make a hole for our big fullback to go smashing through for that single yard to the goal. It seemed logical

to me, but logic doesn't work on the gridiron the way it works in most of life. Perhaps it was just poor logic on my part. It was a mistake and I was as responsible as the coach who failed to send in our place-kicker. In any case, it did not work. Standing on his own goal line and defending seven years of consecutive championships was José María Espinosa de los Monteros. His strength and determination were as great as his name was elegant, and he stopped our fullback as if he were a stone wall. With that tackle he saved the day, a day that had seen three of the most sensational plays ever made on that gridiron: first their successful quarterback sneak early in the first quarter; then our "Statue-of-Liberty" play; and finally that incredible completion of a more than fifty-yard pass on the last play of the game. However, as Yogi Berra is quoted about a baseball game, "It ain't over till its over."

We had performed near miracles, but we did not win the national championship that glorious afternoon in the fall of 1940.

The Lord only knows why we failed to make that extra point. I could easily have become as convinced of my "superiority" as some of those National University students and players whose arrogance I so detested. Instead, I had to be satisfied to have come so close to the national championship and to have been able to complete passes that had been in my dreams for so many years.

Since I had thrown that long pass with only eight seconds left on the clock, the game was over after the failed point after touchdown. As we tried to leave the field, my pass receiver, Juan José Salas, and I had a ridiculous problem. We two could not leave because there was a rather large mob of angry gamblers making ominous threats to

both of us. We could tell that most of them seemed drunk, but what worried us was their great anger. We learned later that some people favoring the National University team had lost great sums of money when they failed to defeat us. At the moment, the fact of having come so close to the championship was uppermost in our minds. We wanted to get home to our families, but mobs are unpredictable, especially when under the influence of alcohol. Security in those days consisted of less than half a dozen policemen and they, too, had no desire to force their way through that angry crowd at the stadium gate. So we just sat there as the excitement of the game faded into the cold aching of our battered bodies in the evening's chill. My mother was still there with some of my brothers and sisters and with my prophetic friend Rafael Lizardi. It was already dark when the mob finally dispersed and we sadly walked to the cars of relatives and friends.

When I was getting into the shower at home, an uncle offered to give me a massage to ease my aches and pains. It was not so much the physical pain of blows that bothered me as it was the mental let down of having come so close to victory without achieving it. When that uncle saw me without clothes and ready for his massage, he said, "Oh my God, you are black and blue from your shoulders to your knees! That did not shock me at all, and I reminded him of the battering those big linesmen had given me all afternoon. He agreed and told me that some of those blows could be heard from the lower part of the stands where he had watched the game. That evening, it seemed very strange to me that my family was so elated, as if we had won, while I felt so dejected. Perhaps that is part of the price that football players pay for participation in high

school and college. The perspective seems to get lost and we therefore give winning or losing too much importance. That is probably why spontaneous games on sandlots or neighborhood fields are more fun. Not that I didn't enjoy the game that afternoon. From the moment our "Statue-of-Liberty" play became successful to the moment that I heard the roar of our student body at the completion of the last pass, I felt the joy of competition against a strong opponent.

That game was commemorated twenty years later when the school voted me a special award for that season's play. It appeared that nobody had equalled my passing record in all those years. The trophy is a happy reminder of my youth. It is also a reminder of the way an entire school started to come out from under the cloud of perceived second-class standing.

Football was not over for me at the end of the 1940 season. I still had one more season to play. Also to be resolved was my vocational dilemma. For the second time in my life I was dreaming of becoming a student at the University of Notre Dame, in the United States. I had no idea at all of playing football for Notre Dame. My size made that an unrealistic expectation and I accepted it. I was only 5 feet 9 inches tall and weighed only 140 pounds. I was too small even for high school football in the U. S., but that didn't bother me at all. I was currently fulfilling my fondest dreams of being a quarterback and of throwing those long spirals with a football. I was also making up for those two years of lost schooling.

Somehow, late in 1941, I found a brochure describing experiments at the University of Notre Dame. That information awakened the almost lost ideal of enrolling at "the

little school back east in South Bend, Indiana that probably accepts Mexicans." The dream was so much renewed that I sent away for their school catalogue. But first, I had to graduate from high school and I had to get good grades. My family could not afford to send me to Notre Dame, and so it was up to me to earn an academic scholarship.

I passed the chemistry exam I had pending. After that I enrolled as a high school senior at Politécnico. I was to take the full senior curriculum plus a repeat course in Analytic Geometry, so it didn't seem possible that I could play any more football. Not if I was to get scholarship-level grades with such an enlarged high school curriculum. It was not just the need for good grades that now drove me. During the 1940 college season of play, our practice field was next to the School of Advanced Biology. As we were finishing those practice sessions, I could see the lights going on in those laboratories. They gave me a sense of yearning for the work going on there, a yearning that had some sadness because I did not know how I could play football and learn all that I wanted to learn in biology. I knew that the team and the student body would expect me to continue as varsity quarterback. I also knew how much time and energy is consumed in college football.

I had been inside those labs many times. I had looked into those beautiful new microscopes and had marveled at the mysteries in those tissues on the slides. Because I was the varsity quarterback and had already given them two high school championships, plus some important college victories, those teachers of Advanced Biology and their students let me study their slides to my heart's content. My vocation was certainly in the biological sciences. The only question was whether I would want to be a research bacte-

riologist or a physician. I had read *The Citadel* by J.C. Cronin, and it had planted the seed of what was to become my vocation in Medicine. I naturally wanted to play on a team declared to be national champions, but I instinctively sensed that I could not play and get scholarship-level grades.

When football practice started in August of 1941, I did not go out for the team. But the team refused to have me absent. They had my brother Carlos as quarterback, but he was only sixteen years old and could only pass with accuracy up to about twenty yards. Carlos was always unorthodox and full of tricks. He established a rather bizarre record in the second game of that season. He called for sixteen consecutive pass plays and completed every one. However, since most of those passes were only for five- or ten-yard gains, the team only scored two touchdowns. Their opponent that afternoon was the Club Wachachara, and they had Julián Amezcua. This time Amezcua did not repeat his foolishness of throwing passes and wasting his running abilities. Carlos established a passing record, but Wachachara won.

The week following this defeat, players, classmates, and even my sisters begged me to return. My teammates and classmates said they needed me. My sisters said I should play to prevent Carlos from getting more of a "swollen head" than he already had. The pressure was too great to deny, and I did want to try again for the national championship. I did not know the meaning of ambivalence at the time. But if a young man was ever ambivalent, I was.

I was also unrealistic. Almost as if the team could expect miracles, I came out for practice only three days before the third game, which was to be against the reign-

ing champions. Our team had a whole new set of plays and I tried to learn them in those three days. Of course, I did not learn them well. It was also impossible to get into good physical condition in such a short period of time, especially to resist the pounding that quarterbacks got. I was expected to complete long passes, as I had done the season before against that same team.

What I did do was receive a lesson about what the Greeks called "hubris," about arrogance. By the middle of the third quarter, I had done exactly the opposite of what my kid brother Carlos had done the Saturday before. I had thrown fifteen passes, all of them incomplete. Coach Mendiola obviously did not want to humiliate me in front of the student body or the hated opponents, and so he did not substitute me, as he normally would have done. I realized that I was failing the team and finally, a bit late, I called time-out and slowly walked off the field. We Mexicans love drama. Even in what was really an embarrassing defeat, we turned it into a football drama. The silence in the stands was, as some wag later called it, deafening. For our opponent's student body it was no great victory to defeat a quarterback they knew was out of practice, and their silence proved that there was no joy in seeing me walk off defeated and humiliated. I felt the utter sadness that only a thoroughly defeated young athlete can feel. As I reached our sideline and my kid brother Carlos came running out, he joked, "Sit down and watch me." A young high school student came down from the stands, jumped the fence, and came out to put his arms around me, sobbing. It was a minor tragedy, but nevertheless that afternoon was a tragedy for me. It is easy to get used to victories and adulation, and I had had too much of both. It is also easy to develop sibling rivalries in sports, and Carlos and I fell into that trap for that whole year. It took age to mellow those foolish feelings of rivalry, but we became very close once we no longer competed against each other. The student who jumped the fence to embrace me in sadness had been my favorite lineman when I coached his junior high school team in 1939. He had only known me in victories. I suppose it was time he found out that I could fail as badly as any quarterback.

What I had to do, of course, was practice regularly, learn my plays, and regain my teammate's confidence. I managed to do all that and to get good grades as well all through 1941. My sense of shame at having passed Analytic Geometry without study prompted me to seek further tutoring from my uncle, the old colonel, and I finished that course with the highest grade possible. All year long I was the number one student in that and in most of my other courses. This time, my efforts were not made to overcome the hostilities of my classmates as in 1933 and 1934 when we returned from California. This time I only wanted to learn the fundamentals of science, and I needed the grades. I spent more hours in those biology labs with those marvelous microscopes than I did on the practice field. Not only did I spend many happy hours over those microscopes, I spent many hours in the small library that was part of the Biological Sciences Department. The mysteries in biology seemed to me far more interesting than the precision and the equations of engineering.

That library was adjacent to the classroom of Dr. Demetrio Sokolov, professor of Logic and Ethics. Dr. Sokolov was already a legend when I first met him the year before. Short and stocky, he spoke with a thick

accent. Two of my best professors, Dr. Sokolov and Dr. Isaac Costero, were refugees from dictator Franco's Spain. There are many reasons why I will always revere the memory of Dr. Demetio Sokolov. That dignified, elderly man personified all that is good about teaching. He was very demanding, and students who came ill-prepared to class were cut off very quickly but always given a chance to improve. Those who gave clear answers—and they had to be clear to satisfy him—got a quick, wry smile and were then asked more advanced questions. It was fascinating to see how logical thought should develop.

My interest in Logic and Ethics was mostly because of the teacher, but parents can influence greatly too. My father never ceased to insist to his eight children that we had to understand and respect logic. He said it was the art of reasoning, and that without it we would only contribute to the foolishness of this world. My dad could be very harsh in his judgments, and I dreaded the thought that he might some day consider me a fool. So it was my respect for my father, as much as the interest that Demetrio Sokolov awakened, that made me interested in the study of logic in particular and in all studies in general.

The football season of 1941 was not a total loss. Before I came out to play, my brother Carlos had not only established that unusual record of sixteen consecutive complete passes, he had also quarterbacked the team to a narrow victory in the first game. Since it was his first game at the college level, he did not even dare throw passes as he did in his next game. Perhaps that was why he completed so many the following week. The opponents didn't consider him a passer, and each time he completed one they probably thought, "Oh, well, that was just luck."

Since he was throwing only short passes, they didn't have time to rush him and he sensed he could continue to complete those short passes.

For the last four games of that season, my mother decided that the team "had to be well fed each game." She knew that a few of our players were from families of such "modest means" that they frequently had no breakfast. We were not so well off ourselves, but my mother's enthusiasm for the game and her love of youngsters prompted her to invite the whole team, coaches and all, to breakfast on the morning of each remaining game. How she managed, I will never know. She had Aurora, a part-time cook, but even so it was a tremendous task to feed more than thirty hungry young people at one time.

It was a boisterous, happy crowd of players and family that gathered those Saturday mornings to eat, to sing, to enjoy life. We naturally became closer friends with everyone on that team. Those breakfasts gave us a feeling of solidarity that probably nothing else could have given us. All those joyful gatherings were enhanced by the presence of my father.

Those young football players and coaches had only read or heard about the tremendous struggle that the Mexican Revolution of 1910 to 1924 had been. They really knew very little about it, just as most people in the northern United States know little about the Civil War as compared to southerners.

One of our players must have asked my father about his experiences in the Revolution because he gave us one of the most vibrant reviews of history I have ever heard. Each Saturday morning as he related his role in that struggle, he truly seemed to be "larger than life." What he

related is in the history books, but his vigorous personality made it come to life. He had been in the middle of that portentous struggle from its very beginning. When only fifteen years old and a student at the National Preparatory School, he had organized a group of twelve students and they had gone off to join Emiliano Zapata, fighting in the hills of Morelos. That lasted only a few days because they were captured and jailed after their first battle.

He had returned to school only to rejoin the Revolution when he was a second-year law-school student. He then won election after election until at age twenty-eight he was elected governor of his state. Finally, with a single speech he had started what the historian Parkes called "the last epic struggle of the first great revolution of the twentieth century." I knew about most of those episodes, but my father was a born story teller and our team was an ideal captive audience for him.

He enjoyed those breakfasts as much or more than my teammates. Even for me, he gave the people's struggle a renewed meaning. We were seeing and hearing a man who had risked his life dozens of times for his ideals.

The sport we were playing had its dangers, but nothing like the dangers he had faced. Hearing him encouraged us immensely. It certainly encouraged me. Ours was a school born of the Revolution, and those true tales of valor told with so much enthusiasm gave us a formidable perspective about our school, our sport, and our nation.

It gave me a firm, almost fierce, determination to be courageous. We began on those Saturdays to understand the dreams and ideals that drove the men and the women of our parents' generation to such tremendous sacrifices. Somewhere in Mexico City there is a house whose walls

must still echo the tales about those giants, those men and women who made the Mexican Revolution possible.

Someone brought a guitar to one of the last breakfasts, and the strains of "La Adelita," a ballad of the Revolution, which we sang with such joy, must surely still resound from those walls. They do in a happy corner of my memories, and those of the whole family.

It was wonderful to be young, even in a "proletarian" school, or perhaps all the more so because we were in the people's school. I felt great pride in being a student at the Politécnico. Having lost two years of schooling, and recalling the refusal by that "Brother" in San Luis Potosi to let me back in school, I firmly believed that being able to go to school was a blessing, a gift from above.

That football season of 1941 ended up with a 14 to 14 tie game against the National University. It was a pretty good game, but nowhere as exciting as our two encounters of the previous year. Both coaches played it cautiously by ordering their quarterbacks to limit passes to a minimum. We were evenly matched and the results proved it. For me, it was a disappointment. Our team had lost the game against Wachachara and I had contributed to our miserable performance and loss in our first game against the National University. It was a let-down, but at least I was happy in my studies. The season was not completely over. I was to have one last chance to throw those long spirals I loved. We were to have our first, and for me the only, international game. Late in November we were to play the El Paso Tigers. This was a high school in El Paso and anybody would naturally think that we should be able to beat them. After all, we had veterans who had played five or six seasons of college football. They had not seen the inside of a classroom in three or four years, but there were no regulations in those days and these veterans just kept on playing. For me, two seasons of college ball satisfied all my dreams except that of leading a college team to a national championship. But the junior high championship in 1938, the high school championship in 1940, and the great college victories in 1940 and 1941 had fulfilled my most important dreams of becoming a good quarterback. And so the game against El Paso was somewhat of an anti-climax for me. Those Texans were all younger than we were, but they more than made up for that by their size. They were so much taller and heavier than us that we knew we were in for a rough afternoon. In a game of constant physical encounters such as football, size can be decisive. It really was a gross mismatch since they outweighed us by more than 20 pounds per man. Those Texas high schools were already in the ethically dubious business of recruiting state and nationwide for their football teams. They also had the advantage of the new T-formation which we had seen only once, the previous year in the second game against the National University. That formation was transforming football throughout the United States, but we were not familiar with it. Our coaches were not allowed money for travel to the so-called "football clinics" in the U.S. until the late 1940s, and thus they were unprepared for what we faced in that Texas team. What was worse, we knew ahead of time that they had a new formation and a very highly regarded passing attack led by a quarterback whose last name I recall was Squires. Sure enough, he literally tore our pass defense to pieces, mostly with little down-and-out passes that we couldn't stop. We put up a valiant enough defense. In November of 1941 the team from Politécnico put up a determined fight against receivers too tall for us to defend and succeeded only in making it an interesting game.

Those giants kicked off to us and we returned to our own 25-yard line. That far from the enemy goal line, they apparently did not expect us to start passing. I decided to give confidence to my team by trying a long pass on the very first down. I knew that they had only vague scouting reports on us because the arrangement to play in Mexico was not made until mid-October. So I figured that they were unaware of my habit of throwing long on the first play of our first possession. It turned out to be true because their safetymen were caught flat-footed when Juan José Salas went breezing straight down the field without any cuts or fakes whatsoever. Juan José reached up and caught my pass of some thirty yards. From deep punt formation I had faded back a little, waiting for Salas to get just beyond their safety, and threw about thirty yards. By this time their big defensive right end had tackled me, but he was inexperienced and therefore hit me around the knees, enabling me to just barely get the pass off in time. With their safety men expecting a running play, Salas just sailed right past them. Just as we had done so many times before in our five seasons together, he didn't even break stride when he reached for the ball, pulled it down out of the sky, and continued running the remaining few yards for a touchdown. That encouraged us enough to hold them to just one touchdown during the entire first half. But they were too big to run against with any measure of success and too tall to complete any but an occasional pass. Even Salas, with his great jumping ability, could not out jump those 6-feet 3-inch and 6-feet 4-inch defenders. I tried every pass in our repertoire and they were able to knock most of them right out of our receiver's hands. We fought to the limit of our abilities. At the half, our coach even appealed to our patriotism!

But it was hopeless. The new T-formation was ringing out all the old formations. Our opponents substituted constantly while we persisted in our coach's entrenched belief of keeping "the best men in." And so I played the entire four quarters without substitution.

The El Paso "Tigers" won 21 to 7.

I knew that I had sent my last long spiral crossing the air over a football field. I had returned my last punt and had quarterbacked my last game. I had fulfilled the best dreams of Chili Beans, that little Mexican kid from the streets of Los Angeles.

In the process I had overcome two major illnesses, heart disease and peritonitis, and had gained an interest in biology. There were other dreams to be fulfilled. I still wanted to become at student at the University of Notre Dame in the States (as we said when referring to the U.S). And that seemed impossible.

The 1941 football season had scarcely ended when the tragedy of Pearl Harbor overtook the world. It made me realize that I would have to study even harder if I was to be able to enroll at a school in the U.S. Because of my heart murmur, I knew that I would probably not be accepted in the armed forces. Nor did I want to be in the middle of a war. But I did want to contribute as a research bacteriologist, or perhaps even as a physician. I was doing very well in my first year of college bacteriology at the Politécnico, but my dream of going to study in South Bend was stronger than ever.

It was not until the fall of 1942, almost a year after Pearl Harbor, that I was given the first glimmer of hope about being accepted to Notre Dame. Two representatives of that university came to interview candidates for scholarships at an elegant place called The University Club, where most U.S. universities had their alumni functions. Until that year, most Mexicans who had been at Notre Dame were from wealthy families. Therefore, it was with high anxiety that I went to this elegant club.

The two persons interviewing candidates for scholarships were the Rev. John A. O'Brien and Professor Paul V. Murray. Father O'Brien seemed mostly interested in the orthodoxy of my faith. I was young and completely trusting on matters of faith. My siblings and I had grown up listening to my dad extolling the merits of the Catholic canon. Not that we understood it all, but we took our father's word for its value as a guide to a way of life. I was able to transmit my father's and my own faith and belief in the Church in my answers to Father O'Brien's questions and that seemed to satisfy him. Paul Murray was a teacher who knew how to speak to young men such as myself. He had lived many years in Mexico where he was now teaching history at the new Mexico City College. Fortunately, he knew a great deal about the Mexican Revolution of 1910-1924 and was a great admirer of my father. Just as I had been lucky to find Dr. Noyola several years before in San Luis, I was now lucky to find Professor Murray at the University Club. He indicated that my grades and credits were good enough to merit a partial scholarship that was available at Notre Dame for Biology majors. The dream of that Mexican boy in the Los Angeles of 1930 was about to come true!

That evening, when I told my mother that this scholarship was available to me, she replied with firm conviction, "If they give you any help at all with such a scholarship, we will see to it that you go to Notre Dame." Her words were so convincing that I felt sure I would soon be a sophomore student at the school of my long-cherished dreams.

A few days later I received notification that the partial scholarship had been awarded me and we began making preparations for the long rail trip to the frozen northlands. My family had enough for the railroad fare, but not enough for the textbooks or laboratory fees. The school catalogue did say that there was a large variety of part-time jobs on campus and that students were free to seek other part-time employment in South Bend. The important thing, I felt, was to get enrolled and settled in a dormitory on that campus. Youth has abundant faith for reaching goals and I had more than enough. So much that I neglected to notice that a formal application for admission had to be filed. And so when I arrived, fascinated by the sight of the golden dome of the university, I was greeted by a very courteous man with a roman collar who looked through the admission files and found that I had indeed been awarded a partial scholarship for entry as a sophomore in the biological sciences, but that I had failed to send an application for acceptance as a student. There I was in the administration building under the golden dome, in the middle of a midwestern snowstorm with my luggage containing most of my worldly possessions. I was more than a thousand miles from home at a university to which I had failed to apply for admission!

That evening I learned my first lesson on how the University of Notre Dame treats strangers. That religious brother recognized my confusion and ignorance of school systems in the U.S. and simply said, "You have come a long way. You do have the award of a partial scholarship, and I'm not going to send you all the way back to Mexico. Since you have no relatives or friends who could put you up temporarily while applications are processed, let's process the application right now." It took awhile, for there were several pages of questions and information to fill out, but with his help I filled everything out. He smiled and said something about my now being a student at the University of Notre Dame. Little did he know what a long and at times seemingly impossible odyssey it had been.

Since that day long ago in Los Angeles, when John Worth had dashed my hopes of going to U.S.C. or to U.C.L.A. and George LaPorte had told me about "a little school back east in South Bend," I had alternated between hope and despair. Now, here I was, finally enrolled under the golden dome.

I had arrived in the middle of winter and in the middle of World War II. Everybody there was so rushed and so worried about relatives in the armed forces or their own imminent entry into the war that a confused foreign student would have to figure everything out for himself. Those were rather sad times, with lists of "Missing in Action" posted almost every week on our dormitory bulletin board. The battle of Guadalcanal was on and not going very well. It was clear that Americans were more worried about the war in the Pacific than the battles in North Africa and Europe. It was dangerous to be young. The youth of the world were being slaughtered.

Morning mass in our dormitory chapel took on a new meaning for someone such as I who had never been near

war. I had known about revolution on the border when my father was running his very real risks in 1929 and again during his conspiracies of 1940. But this time, in 1943, everybody around me was affected in one way or another. Everything seemed to be done in a hurry, so much so that a pair of students from Colombia said to me that they could not understand Yankees because they were always on the run and yet always left saying, "Take it easy."

These South Americans did not identify with the suffering nation as I did. After all, I had grown up in Texas and California. I felt very much a Mexican, but somehow I felt that the United States was my country, too. How could I not feel that the worry and the pain that surrounded me was also mine?

The war changed everything. There was strict food rationing and the dining-room food was an unpleasant surprise. I was used to warm breakfasts and lunches at home in Mexico. But at Notre Dame I had to get used to a breakfast of cold milk with cornflakes or cold milk with oatmeal, coffee without cream and usually without sugar, and cold slices of ham or tasteless chicken for lunch and dinner. Mealtimes were so unappealing that they became more of an interruption of my hectic schedule than anything else. And hectic it certainly was. I had enough credits to be rated as a sophomore, but I also lacked two freshman courses that had to be added to my schedule: Freshman English and Freshman Chemistry.

The most noticeable change from the school system in Mexico and the one at Notre Dame was the pace. We were on a wartime-accelerated track. This demanded accumulation of knowledge made more difficult with the three jobs I had to meet my expenses. The jobs and the two

extra freshman courses proved to be too much stress for my otherwise young body. The course in Freshman English was given by Brother Pat, the same one who had admitted me without an application on the night of my arrival. He was a good teacher and I came to appreciate English literature for the first time.

The laboratories were just as fascinating as the ones in Mexico, with the added incentive that they were the site of the discovery of synthetic rubber by Father Neiuland, who was naturally a campus legend. Those chemistry labs had the peculiar odor that old labs used to have, and I loved them. Sophomore biology consisted of lectures and was limited to the study of theory. I was engrossed in the subject, but the second semester, with dissections of various species of animals, was more intriguing.

The stress of so much work, the pace required, and the skipping of meals produced the inevitable and resulted in my getting a duodenal ulcer. The pain in the pit of my stomach started at what I thought an appropriate time. It started suddenly and severely at about three in the afternoon on Good Friday of 1943. At the end of the liturgy, when the priest in the main campus church recalled the death of Christ on the cross and closed the book with loud finality, all the church lights were put out and the candles snuffed out too. In that silence and darkness, although surrounded by fellow students, I felt utterly alone.

Only God knows why I felt so lonely. I went back to my dorm with the pain in my stomach. The next day I had black stools, which I knew must be a sign of something bad, such as bleeding from the stomach. Preparing for Easter, I went for a haircut on campus the next day and was shocked to see how skinny my neck looked in the bar-

ber's mirror. I knew I was in some danger and went to see the Dean of Science the following Monday. He, too, expressed concern. He declared that I had to drop at least one sophomore course and two of my part-time jobs. But first he said I had to go to the student infirmary. He also gave me a note to take to Father William F. Cunningham, unofficial counselor to Latin American students. There was no doctor available at the infirmary because of the wartime shortage of physicians, but Father Cunningham turned out to be my salvation. He took me to St. Joseph's Hospital in South Bend and arranged for my care.

I was discharged from the Hospital in less than a week and Father Cunningham came for me and took me to the Mission House on campus. There on the edge of one of the two lakes of that beautiful campus, I was given the job that Knute Rockne once had when he was a student. It consisted of "taking care of the Log Chapel" and helping with the housework at the Mission House. This house was where the priests of that order came to recuperate from their stints as missionaries in Bengal, India. It was the only place on campus where the food was not rationed and I learned to eat slowly. I also became acquainted with the pleasure of strawberries with whipped cream.

Every evening after sweeping out the little chapel and making sure the vigil light was on, the missals were on the two altars and opened to the place for the next morning's masses, and that the vestments of the correct color were in place, I would sit alone there for a while. Somehow I no longer felt lonely nor did I feel nostalgia for Mexico. Without advice and without knowing fully what I was doing, I learned the value of meditation. Sitting there in front of that image of the crucified Christ, I realized how good

life was. I regained my faith in myself and I finally realized my vocation. I decided I would become a physician.

It is a strange fact of life for some of us that the counsels of despair become the instruments of motivation. I had already overcome two serious illnesses and returned to school and to sports. Now I had another obstacle. Duodenal ulcers, by the very type of personalities that usually suffer them, have a strong tendency to recur and to bleed again and again. One warm lazy summer afternoon I was resting in my room at the Mission House. I had my window open and could hear two missionary priests chatting on the front porch less than three yards from my open window. They were talking about me, believing me to be asleep. The older of the two said something to the effect that my idea of becoming a physician was beyond my reach. I recall the sadness in his voice when he said, "Poor boy, he already has a bad heart and now he has a bleeding ulcer, I don't see how he can expect to become a doctor." The other, younger priest was Father Charles Callahan and he answered that I had already shown enough determination to overcome serious obstacles and that he felt sure I could overcome this latest problem. Normally, the negative assessment of the older priest would have been accurate, but in my case it was Father Callahan who made the right prophecy. Some five years later he was to hear my confession on the night before Luz María Dávila and I were married at that Log Chapel. By that time I had finished medical school and was doing my internship in Mexico City. Luz María and I, with help from Dr. Lawrence Rossi, had eloped from Mexico to the U.S. in order to get married at that little chapel. Lawrence Rossi was my classmate at the National University School of Medicine. He was from Peking, Illinois, across the river from Peoria, and was able to arrange that I work for one month as an intern in St. Francis Hospital in Peoria.

I learned a great deal of obstetrics in that month and earned all of $75, with which we got married. Luz María lived that month at the Rossi family home across the Illinois river. She had learned enough English during my years as a medical student to understand and enjoy the language. She also saw what a midwestern winter was like, since the month I worked at St. Francis was January of 1949.

After the ulcer had healed in the summer of 1943, I still stayed on for one more semester at Notre Dame. It was not easy to leave those wonderful laboratories, but my mind was made up. Those quiet moments in the log chapel had given me the needed strength.

February 29, 1944 was my first day as a medical student at the National University in Mexico City. My parents could not possibly afford medical school costs in the U.S. They had a hard time paying my way through school just in Mexico. I usually lacked most of my textbooks in my years as a medical student, but there were medical libraries I could use.

Medical school, especially the first year, is an arduous and stressful experience. It can be grim and discouraging because of the impossible amount of scientific data a student is expected to learn. Even lacking the textbooks during that first year, it was nevertheless a wonderful year for me. On that first day as a medical student, right after the 4 p.m. class, I went to the ancient suburb of Coyoacán and had my first date with my future wife, Luz María Dávila. We went to a little park called Chimalixtac, in front of an abandoned sixteenth-century chapel. Life

changed entirely for me on that day because I was able to bring myself to express my love for her. Her beauty and good humor had impressed me for several years, but I truly did not believe that any girl as beautiful as Luz María could possibly fall in love with me.

She was six years younger than I and I hardly knew how to express my feelings. I spoke to her not only of my love, but I also told her that I did not intend to stay and become another Mexico City physician. That city already had too many doctors and I wanted to work where I would be needed. I told Luz María that I intended to go to the United States to serve the Mexican farm workers laboring in the fields of the Imperial Valley of California. I knew of their great need and was determined to work for them. I had to tell Luz María of these plans because I knew her family would naturally prefer to have her stay in her own country. I did not want my plans to come as a surprise to her or to her family. If we were to pledge our love, it had to be with full knowledge of what my plans for the practice of medicine would require. It is seldom easy to emigrate from one country to another. In 1944, Mexico City was a delightful city to live in and it was going to seem to her mother that leaving it was almost absurd.

Luz María must have had complete faith in my ability to get through medical school because she proceeded without any suggestion from me to enroll in English classes that same month of February.

I was, to put it mildly, dreadfully afraid of the final examination in the first year's course of Descriptive Human Anatomy. That course had the ominous reputation of failing approximately fifty percent of all who took the exam. At age 25, I could not afford to fail. With borrowed

books and using the medical-school library, I was able to make good progress. The knowledge that such a beautiful girl was in love with me made the arduous work of first-year medical school not only worthwhile but also a very happy year.

All the dreams that a microscope had first awakened in me were revived. The mystery of cells making up a human body became progressively attractive. Our class in Anatomy was so large that each student had only two or three opportunities in the whole year to demonstrate his or her knowledge of the subject. My first turn came near the middle of the year, and I had to get up in front of my class and, with a stern professor looking on, recite my allotted six pages of descriptive human anatomy. It was almost certainly my only chance to express my knowledge in the whole year, so it had to be well done. I had prepared for it and even with some stuttering at the very beginning pulled it off with flying colors. My subject that day was "Arteries, Nerves and Veins of the Human Heart." Not a simple one, to be sure. But being an old cardiac patient myself, I had prepared it with precision and knew it well.

Between that stern professor and Luz María, the study of medicine became a voyage of fascinating discoveries. The study of medicine has much that is tedious work, but for me it was a fulfillment of a young man's almost impossible dreams. Mexico City and the old suburbs of Coyoacan and San Angel were as romantic a setting as anyone would wish to live in. I carried with me my dissection scissors (properly disinfected, of course) and used them to reach over fences into the gardens of San Angel to cut roses for Luz María. Those narrow sixteenth-century streets and alleys of Coyoacan and San Angel had

once echoed the footstep of Hernán Cortez and his fellow conquistadors, and now they echoed the footsteps of a young couple in love. In love and dreaming of the practice of medicine and the raising of a family in what is for most Mexicans the most foreign of nations: the United States of America.

Not that there was much time for romance. The setting was right, but medical school was a burden so heavy that students writing about it invariably declare it to be almost unbearable. There was certainly no time for any further football playing for me. Time and energy had to be spent in learning as much medicine as possible and I did not expect to participate in football, except as a spectator.

Fate was to intervene and put me right in the middle of one of the most interesting episodes in the history of American football in Mexico. I was to participate in what is still remembered as "La leyenda del Padre Lambert" (The legend of Father Lambert). For legend it has become. The story of Father Lambert is a rare saga of victories where defeat had become almost the norm. It is also the story of how much influence one good, decent man can have over an entire city. For Lambert J. Dehner, O.S.B. was a most extraordinary man. Especially considering that he had always seen himself as being just ordinary.

It all started when I was doing my second year of medical school at the National University. I was at my desk in the bedroom I shared with my brother Carlos, trying to understand Human Physiology, when he burst in with startling news.

"I have found a new football coach for the Politécnico, and he is a Gringo. Now we will finally win the national championship."

"Big deal. The National University still has that Gringo coach from Yale."

"Yes, they have, but this Gringo is a Roman Catholic priest and he played under one of Knute Rockne's last halfbacks and everyone here will associate him with Notre Dame football!"

I then tried to tell him that it was absolutely out of the question because the Politécnico was a state school and the separation of Church and State was nowhere more vehement than it was in Mexico. The Secretariat of Public Education would certainly not authorize a coach's salary to a Catholic priest. Carlos replied that the Benedictan order, to which Lambert Dehner belonged, was willing to continue paying him his full stipend as a teacher at a local Catholic high school. He was to continue teaching some classes there but would be permitted to work full-time as a coach at the Politécnico. Father Lambert's superior in Kansas obviously believed that as a football coach at a large school such as the Politécnico, Lambert would exert a lasting, positive influence.

Somehow, we were able to keep his religious status a secret for several weeks, long enough for the school to furnish the uniforms and to accept the volunteer from up north as head coach. The fact that priests were not even allowed to wear their Roman collars in public helped to make the ruse work long enough to get us past our first game. By then the enthusiasm for having Lambert Dehner as head coach had become so pervasive that the Secretary of Public Education would have been faced with a widespread student rebellion if he had displaced our new coach.

Carlos had gone around that huge campus, where he had once attended a few classes and shops, convincing students that Father Lambert J. Dehner would lead us to our first national championship. His wild prophecy came true: students and fans did associate Father Lambert with Notre Dame! It frustrated Lambert greatly to have to explain over and over again that his association had only been that of a player at St. Benedict's College where the head coach was "Moon" Mullins, one of Knute Rockne's last Notre Dame backfield players. Finally, we convinced him to give up explaining and accept that he was perceived as coming from "The Fighting Irish." He never accepted this innocent deception because he did not consider it innocent. His string of victories were enough evidence to most that he came from the fountain of football greatness and was transmitting it to us.

I was caught up in that hopeful atmosphere too. I accepted the role of "Assistant Coach for the Backfield" at the Politécnico. There was no salary for me there, so I was accepted as a volunteer. It was a bit awkward for me because I was a student at the University that was the Politécnico's main rival. I did not see it as a conflict of interest since my football loyalty would always have to be with Politécnico. I was enrolled in the University Medical School only because the degree from the School of Rural Medicine at the Politécnico was not recognized outside of Mexico and I intended to work as a physician for migrants in the U.S.

I was really more of a personal translator for the good padre than anything else. As he developed his language ability in Spanish, I became more of a backfield coach.

Lambert's personality more than made up for his faltering Spanish in those early months of the season of 1945. He had a disciplined, orderly way of thinking things out

and a truly profound understanding of how young men react under stress. He was under great stress himself in trying to understand the contradictions of Mexican character. He was used to the orderly way of life in a Benedictine Monastery. The passionate and somewhat disorderly way of life of the average Mexican male was a source of constant frustration for Father Lambert. He survived that strange society and changed it, perhaps more than he ever realized. He was more perceptive and certainly much more tolerant of our way of life than the average Gringo tourist.

He understood early on that the greatest obstacle to more decisive football victories was the poor self-esteem that most of our students and players still had. The Politécnico had briefly come out of the doldrums of feeling "second class" with the triumphs of 1940. However, we had not achieved the national championship and we desperately needed it to confirm our sense of equality with the National University. When Lambert came on as head coach, our main rival had been the national champion for twelve consecutive years!

The attraction that Lambert provoked was so widespread and sincere that I recall how his personality caused us to have a faith in success which was so strong that it continually grew and fed on itself. We seemed to sense that this was the change we had been looking for. It was something as intangible as it was contagious. Fortunately for the Politécnico, the regulations about eligibility were actually non-existent. Some of our players on that 1945 team had not seen the inside of a classroom in three or four years. There is no question that football is capable of provoking true obsession.

The rivalry with the National University had become

so passionate that it caused in us a vehement desire to defeat them again. We wanted more than simple victories, we wanted the National championship. Oh how we wanted that championship!

I had a reputation for a level head on the playing field, but in 1945 I was crazy enough to take time from my medical studies in order to coach with Father Lambert on those sidelines.

Mexicans, in general, are prone to be passionate. We certainly love the dramatic, and football lends itself to drama. We were just as guilty of exaggerating the importance of this game as the towns in Texas that go crazy every Friday night during football season. The difference was that those townspeople in places such as Odessa and Midland, Texas have money to spend on their teams and we barely had enough for uniforms and football shoes.

We didn't need money to recruit players, however. The hopes raised by the appearance of Lambert Dehner on our practice field were enough to give us an abundance of experienced players.

Lambert's personality contributed greatly to his ultimate success. He was young and vigorous. He looked strong, and he was indeed as strong in character as he was in physical appearance.

He needed strength because Lambert J. Dehner, O.S.B. was coping with a society that was so different from what he was accustomed to that he had to feel alienation and frequent anger. Even the language obstacle was a serious one. It took most of that first season before he was able to make his Spanish understood.

During one of our early practice sessions he took me aside and asked, "How do you say 'get the lead out of your

pants' in Spanish?"

He didn't understand the language, but he certainly understood our psychology. He understood our hunger. Best of all was the fact that he enjoyed being coach at the working-class school."

From the first day of practice we all sensed a feeling of excitement. It was noticeable on the field and in the schools of that huge campus. There were more spectators at many of our practice scrimmages of 1945 than we had had at some of our 1939 championship games!

Father Lambert represented a radical change of attitudes. Finding out that he was a Catholic priest—as everyone seemed to learn the day of our first game—added a certain mystery for most students and fans.

The day before that first game, as he called a halt to the practice session, Father Lambert brought the team together and told me to announce to them that the following day he would officiate at "the Holy Sacrifice of the Mass" at the main altar of the Basilica of Our Lady of Guadalupe." That, of course, is Mexico's most important shrine, and the announcement surprised all of us, including myself. It is not easy for a foreign priest to be allowed to offer mass there, except under special circumstances. Lambert Dehner was wise. He knew that offering mass there with the whole team present would send a clear message concerning the moral behavior he expected from all of us. He didn't have to know the language. He was not the type to rely on preaching either. He simply did things and expected us to understand them.

When he announced the mass of the following day, one of our best linemen confronted me with some anger. He was angry because I had not told him that Lambert was

a priest, and this player had been swearing throughout every practice scrimmage. I simply told him that it was time he watched his foul mouth, anyway.

The next morning at mass I was supposed to assist Lambert with the Latin responses and all the other functions of a regular altar boy. I knew the responses, but I was so amazed at being so close to the mantle with Our Lady's image that I rang the bells at the Epistle (very early in the mass). Lambert just smiled and said, "Not yet." It was one of the unique and happy experiences of my life to serve at mass on that altar. I suppose only Mexicans can fully understand what that shrine means to a whole nation. The Spaniards came to conquer and found in the natives of Mexico a spirituality so strong that it still amazes most visitors. It is a spirituality that unites us more than anything else in our history. I felt like a nervous, happy kid that day at the altar. And we all felt sure that we would win.

There was much more than language that needed cleaning up at the Instituto Politécnico of 1945. What Lambert Dehner inherited when he started coaching there was a motley crew of veterans and about two dozen eager young student players. Of the twenty-two veterans, almost half, including my brother Carlos, had not been students for several years. Of course, our opponents had a similar situation. Their team was also a mixture of "fossils" and regular students.

This lack of regulations bothered Lambert, but not as much as the pervasive attitudes of machismo of so many of our players and our male students. That display of flamboyant, arrogant manliness is one of the worst vices of Mexican males. It shows up almost everywhere and was much more prevalent in 1945 than it is today. Mexican women, like the women of most of this planet, have had their fill of that senseless arrogance and it is slowly losing strength.

One of the traits that seems to go with *machismo* is a lack of discipline. Lambert put an end to that by keeping "star" players who had failed to show up for some practice sessions on the bench for the next championship game. They thought they were indispensable and *muy machos,* and they were shocked when Lambert benched them.

The new coach demanded discipline and obtained it by keeping these "stars" on the bench whenever they missed a practice without a reasonable excuse. Not only did this bring those young men in line, it also gave some younger and inexperienced players a chance to play in championship games.

At that time there was no system of using certain players for offense and another set of players exclusively for defense. This is now called "platooning," and it creates specialists who can only play on offense or defense. Father Lambert instituted his own type of platooning. From the very first game he started sending in groups of three, four, or more fresh players at odd moments. He did this on offense as well as when we were on defense, and that achieved great success. First of all, it surprised our opponents as they saw a constant change of new faces confronting them. It also conveyed the clear message to our players that they all had a chance to play and were expected to know both offensive and defensive formations.

This made for a constant supply of fresh and eager players. It thoroughly confused all our opponents, just as it enhanced the morale of our team. Those veteran "stars" lost their presumed security and had to hustle to get more

time on the field of play.

There was very little complaining from players. No longer were minor injuries the cause of whining, and, by the same token, nobody felt they had to stay on the field when injured just to prove their manliness. Every one of our players simply wanted to play on the team they felt sure would finally win the first national championship for the Politécnico.

Long before the last game, school spirit had been visibly uplifted. That season was a whole new type of football for me. Each time Lambert indicated that I send in fresh substitutes, I would go to the bench and call out the names of the backfield players to enter the game. When I called for players with little game experience, they would look at me with a mixture of surprise first and then, as I told them "get in there," I could see their surprise turn into a fierce determination to do battle.

They needed no rallies, no coaches exhorting them the day before to "die for dear old Politécnico." All they needed was a chance to play, and everybody got their chance. In critical games we kept the more experienced players in more than in other games, of course. But we always substituted more often than our opponents. No longer did our team slow down in the last quarter of games, as we generally had done during my playing days. It was exciting to coach with this system of constant substitutions.

Because of the score accumulation system in use that year, we had to play against the National University three times! The first encounter was won by them on a technicality. My brother Carlos was quarterbacking most of the game and called an unorthodox play that the sportswriters called "the hidden end." With less than a minute to play in the last quarter, and with the track that surrounded the gridiron filled with spectators, Carlos pulled one of his trick plays. He called for a time-out to explain to our right end to stay kneeling near the side line after the next play. Then he called a running play to the right side followed by another to the left. After the first of these two, our right end stayed just inside the field, kneeling and hardly visible because he was blending in with the crowd that had jumped down from the stands and was on the track just behind our player. Thus, on third down, with the ball in our possession way over to the other side of the field, Carlos took the ball from center and threw to our "hidden end" far over on the other side of the field. Nobody had noticed the absence of our player from the line on this third play; nobody had counted our players on the line either. And so our right end was all alone when he took in the short pass from Carlos and easily ran the fifteen or twenty yards to a touchdown. The rules had nothing about such a trick play. There were no regulations or security guards keeping the public in the stands, and the anger it produced in our opponents, as well as in the thousands of fans on the other side of the stadium, was more than understandable. The turmoil was so great that a mob of our opponents surrounded the head linesman and intimidated him into calling a penalty against us. He did this by ruling that one of our two ends did not have a three-point stance on the line, as was required in those days. Since the referee was so confused that he had not yet raised his hands indicating a touchdown, the ruling by the linesman had to be accepted and that canceled our touchdown. We could not prove that all our linemen had a three-point stance with

both feet on or no more then half a yard from the line of scrimmage and one hand on the ground. Carlos called for one more pass, but there was so much anger and confusion on our side that the receivers failed to run their patterns and the pass was incomplete. The National University was declared the winner and a riot broke out. The last I saw of that head linesman, he was running for his life with his shirt torn off, near the gate where four or five policemen would, presumably, save him.

After that bizarre ending, we still had six or seven games to play, including an "international game" against a Texas high school. We went on to win every one of those games, as Father Lambert's mystique seemed to permeate the team and students.

The game against a Houston high school gave Mexico its first international victory. True, this victory of ours was against players generally younger than ours—we had seven or eight veterans with more than four seasons of play—but the rest of our team was made up of legitimate, young students. Furthermore, those Texans had the advantage of sheer size. They looked like giants, and they were giants. They averaged six feet in height and their weight was at least fifteen to twenty pounds greater than any of our players. It was no small thing for us to defeat those young giants. We had been grossly mismatched when we played that team from El Paso, Texas in 1942. It is true that by 1945 we had more big men on the team, but the main difference was that the T-formation was no longer a mystery or a surprise to us. Above all, the difference was Lambert J. Dehner.

Our second game against the National University was a masterpiece of teamwork and enthusiasm. Even lacking

our quarterback Carlos, who was out with a knee injury, we felt sure of victory. We blocked and we tackled with the fury of determination. We executed plays from three different formations, almost without a flaw. We felt like winners and played like winners. Lambert, with all of his innovations, was still old-fashioned in that he did not emphasize the passing game. He didn't need to in order to win. There was not a single touchdown pass thrown that day. A few short passes were completed, but we made most of our gains by running. We had Manuel "Pibe" Vallari in our backfield, and he was probably the best running back in the history of football in Mexico. He also was the most dangerous punt returner ever. So we relied on the running game and won 24 to 7. That was the most decisive defeat that the National University had ever suffered.

The third and final game against that the National University was early in November. That game made history in more ways than one. The buses that we rented to take us to the National Stadium were old and dilapidated, so old that one of them, carrying Father Lambert and most of our backfield players as well as myself, broke down right in the middle of busy Insurgentes Avenue. We were left high and dry about two miles from the stadium. Lambert ordered "everybody out to push this junk out of traffic." Our players already had their pads, uniforms, and cleated shoes on. This was because we knew that the old National Stadium had no dressing rooms or showers. I started to object that our backfield players would exert themselves too much pushing that heavy bus. Lambert just laughed at this idea of mine and then with some anger said to me, "Where in hell did you ever get the idea that backfield players are more important than linesmen?" That, of course, endeared him even more to our linesmen. I looked more than a bit ridiculous with that foolish objection, but by the same token it let the backfield men know how much I cared for their well-being. Walking the ten or twelve city blocks we had to walk that afternoon, with the high cleats used in the football shoes of the time, on cement sidewalks, left all our players with sore feet. Nevertheless, it helped us more than it hurt us because it gave us a chance to sing like warriors on the way to the battlefield.

Everybody, including Lambert and me, pushed that old junk to the other side of Insurgentes Avenue. We then went walking, sounding somewhat like horses do on city streets with our long cleats ringing on those cement sidewalks. Somebody started singing and soon the block-long line of football players in clean new uniforms was singing and joking. Suddenly we had a huge crowd of people following us and singing with us. We sang as if we had already won the game. Someone had translated "Anchors Aweigh," and we sang it with a vengeance. The same joy went into a translated Notre Dame "Victory March." We felt that we were on our way to becoming national champions, and we marched and sang with the joy and abandon that only young athletes feel on their way to great challenges.

We knew we were going to play a good team. The lopsided victory of the second game was due to near perfect execution by all of our players, but we didn't really expect to win by three touchdowns as we had in that game. We had our first- and second-string quarterbacks out with injuries. In fact, we had a significant number of injuries from our game against those Texas giants. But somehow we had the conviction that we were going to win. They

had been national champions for twelve consecutive years, but we had proven that we could defeat them decisively. Furthermore, as one of our players pointed out to me between songs, "We went to petition Our Lady of Guadalupe just this morning, and we are going to win."

During the rest of that long walk I, too, felt that Our Lady of Guadalupe couldn't possible fail to help us. After all, I rationalized, those arrogant University snobs didn't take the trouble to go to the fountain of our faith. So we were going to battle arrogance and heresy! At least that is how we felt on that march to our final victory.

It was a victory by just one point, 21 to 20, but a victory nevertheless. Without our two best quarterbacks, we lacked a good passing attack. That made for an even match. That afternoon, more than at any other game, Lambert's strategy of giving every player game experience paid off. It proved to be our salvation because the missing and injured players had to have replacements with some experience. The blocking and tackling were fierce, just as it had been in those "classics" between our two teams in 1940.

I felt young and full of energy just watching my backfield players perform so well. The National University threw two dozen passes in that game and only completed three, none for a touchdown. When Pibe Vallarie returned an enemy punt sixty-five yards for a touchdown late in the last quarter, we felt that we had won. We were ahead 13 to 6 with less than three minutes of play left.

We were sure we could contain them. But they were defending the prestige of so many years as champions and they somehow managed to smash down the field with only one short pass and a desperate running attack that brought them a touchdown. That made it 13 to 12. Just as we had

been in 1940, now they were one point away from a tie game which would have forced a playoff. We couldn't afford a tie because we had so many injured players. We had to block their kick for the point after touchdown. As the other team was in the huddle, Lambert sent in a player with instructions. He wanted our left end, Uriel González, a Texan and our only player over six feet tall, to get right up against our left tackle and thus closer to the opponent who was to try kicking that point-after. I also had him wave his hands high over his head. We wanted to intimidate our opponents with the possibility of a blocked kick by our giant end. The ploy worked! The opponent's quarterback changed the mark where he was going to set the football for his kicker. Since the clock did not continue to run after a touchdown, their quarterback had time to whisper something to his kicker. He later told me that he had told his kicker that Uriel was too far in and that he, the kicker, should aim to the left because that giant end was going to come in from the right side. So he changed his mark and thereby lost the game and the championship. The kicker followed instructions just a little bit too well. His kick hit the left upright post and bounced back into the end zone.

Now it was not only the roar of the crowd that was awesome. I turned from the bench to look at our side of the stadium and saw that most of those thousands of students and fans had newspapers in their hands, twisted and lighted like torches. The sun was setting on that western side of the stadium and the sky was an orange red. The fire from those torches made the sky look even redder. Such had never happened in any stadium in Mexico, and it was as dangerous as it was exciting. It was a sight to bring balm to what had once been a damaged heart—mine. Someone had distributed leaflets with a most appropriate and humorous folk song about chopping down the tree where the bird of paradise (the National University, of course) had lived and now would have to sleep on the ground "JUST LIKE ANY OTHER ANIMAL." The singing was so loud and joyous that I turned to Father Lambert and asked him if he thought that we would "wake up the echoes" He was as happy as anyone in the stadium. He had done more than he realized for the spiritual sense of so many people in our struggling, tumultuous society. We did wake up the echoes: Echoes of so many years of cheering and jeering from our proud opponents; echoes of great victories without the championship. The working-class people of Mexico City finally had their school as a national sports champion.

My mother was so overjoyed that she told us afterwards that as soon as she realized we had won, she embraced a policeman standing nearby! For some it was not just a sport victory. For many of us it was a dream come true.

We didn't realize at the time that we became champions because we had become better persons. We had been able to perceive that it is better to be decent than to be *muy macho*. In a city, indeed in a whole nation plagued by *machismo*, decency was once again seen as our ancestors had seen it, as a primary virtue.

In the process, our students had become better athletes. And we were better athletes because we became disciplined.

Lambert J. Dehner, O.S.B. performed near miracles that year of 1945. I know because I had been at the

Politécnico since it's founding in 1938 and saw the differences. He renewed our faith in ourselves, just as he renewed our respect for the spiritual values that lie hidden in the soul of every true Mexican. Going to the Shrine of Our Lady of Guadalupe on the day of important games was not a superstitious gesture, as some would have us think. But those who are that cynical just don't understand Mexico. The change in values that Lambert brought about was at first almost imperceptible. I had played under the old system and had a basis for comparison. Not that there was great immorality in the team or the school before Lambert came to coach. Our previous coach, Señor Salvador Mendiola, was certainly a decent and very thoughtful man. And he knew football as well as Lambert. It was the general attitude of the team and of Mexico City society, in all its social classes, that had degenerated into a pervasive *machismo*. Mexican women, in many cases, believed they had to tolerate it. They tempered or balanced it's brutality by instilling religion in their sons, their brothers, and every male they could influence.

In 1945 we needed to see—as we did in that young priest—how vigorous and wholesome a disciplined life can make a man. We needed to be reminded—as my mother constantly did with me and my brothers—of the truth in the old Mexican adage, "*Lo cortes no quita lo valiente.*" ("Courtesy does not diminish courage".)

Before Lambert Dehner came, the Politécnico team used to gather just before the opening kickoff of every game, hold hands, and shout obscenities about courage. When Lambert came on, we gathered at the sideline and said a short prayer. We prayed for victory, of course, but we also prayed that there be no injuries on our team or on our opponent's. Everybody soon learned that what we did in those ritualistic gathering of players and coaches was pray. It was simple and without embarrassment. We had developed a more serene attitude towards football. We had the same passion with less vehemence and with more joy.

We were hungry for decency and didn't know it. This was true of the school as much as of our team. For us, Lambert J. Dehner represented all that was decent. The teams I had played on in 1938 to 1941 were made up of athletes as good as those of 1945. The difference was in the intangibles, such as self-esteem. We, of course, did not realize how much we had changed. But we certainly had. We were real winners. We already knew that the Politécnico was a good school. Now we were happy as the national champions of 1945.

From the day when I had first seen a football sailing across the California skies to that last game in 1945, I had many reasons to be grateful for the great game of football.

I did not play football "in the pursuit of excellence," as some coaches and writers would have young men believe. Nor did I play it to prove that my cardiologists were wrong. It is true that I played it partly to prove that I was not a cardiac invalid, but I played it more because I enjoyed it. I played it for the sheer joy of throwing long spiral passes.

Finally, I played it not for the winning of championships, local or national. I played it because it was fun.